I READ to Write

PREPARING for WRITING ASSESSMENTS

3

TEACHER EDITION

CONTENT AREAS: MATH • SCIENCE • SOCIAL STUDIES

ZB Zaner-Bloser

Program Reviewers

Zaner-Bloser wishes to thank these educators who reviewed portions of this program and provided comments prior to publication.

Debra Andries
K–5 Literacy Specialist
Minneapolis Public Schools
Minneapolis, Minnesota

Tracy Britton
Science Teacher
Strongsville City Schools
Strongsville, Ohio

Catherine Cassy
Curriculum Specialist
St. Louis Public Schools
St. Louis, Missouri

Myra Collins
Curriculum Consultant—Math
NE Missouri Regional Professional Development Center
Kirksville, Missouri

Elizabeth Ference
Graduate Instructor, Retired
Department of Curriculum and Instruction
Judith Herb College of Education
University of Toledo
Toledo, Ohio

Karen R. Hammons
Instructional Supervisor
Bath County
Owingsville, Kentucky

Kristin Marsala Matsis
Teacher
Bullis Charter School
Los Altos, California

Antonio Rodriguez
Curriculum Specialist—STEM
Milwaukee Public Schools
Milwaukee, Wisconsin

Consultant: James Scott Miller, M.Ed.

I Read to Write was developed with assistance from Gare Thompson and Pegeen Wright.

Photo Credits: Cover: (tree trunk), © iStock.com/Thomas Demarczyk, (thunderstorm), © iStock.com/SVphotography, (cliff palace) © iStock.com/snoofek; p. Z15 (iPad), © Courtesy of Logitech; pp. T4 (background), T6, © shmel/iStock; p. T7, NOAA/NWS; p. T10, © Leemage/Getty Images; p. T18, T24–T25, © 2/Andrew Holt/Ocean/Corbis; pp. T20–T21, © Mark Sykes/JAI/Corbis; p. T25 (top), © Hulton-Deutsch Collection/Corbis; pp. T32–T33, T38–T39, © Jon Hicks/Corbis

Art Credits: pp. T6, T10, T34 (grass), Zaner-Bloser; pp. T4, T11 (Fahrenheit), Tracy Greenwalt; p. T25, Inspiré de l'Image: Anasazi Map USA1.GIF; pp. T32 (garden), T34 (garden), T39, Rob Schuster

ISBN 978-1-4531-1582-4

Copyright © 2016 Zaner-Bloser, Inc.

Zaner-Bloser, Inc.
1-800-421-3018
www.zaner-bloser.com
Printed in the United States of America

3 4 5 6 7 8 9 10 11 12 23975 21 20 19 18 17 16

ZB Code 16

SUSTAINABLE FORESTRY INITIATIVE   Certified Sourcing
www.sfiprogram.org
SFI-00959

TABLE OF CONTENTS

I READ to Write

PREPARING for WRITING ASSESSMENTS

I Read to Write: Responding to Sources is a simple, flexible solution that helps students master the skills needed for close reading and responding to multiple sources on writing assessments.

With *I Read to Write,* students learn to

✔ **read closely across tests**—with appropriate scaffolding—to analyze text structures and acquire a deeper understanding of texts.

✔ **cite text evidence** as they **respond to multiple sources** in writing.

✔ **write across content areas** (Science, Social Studies, and Math) and within **three text types:** Narrative, Informative/Explanatory, and Opinion.

✔ **practice skills essential to success on next generation assessments.**

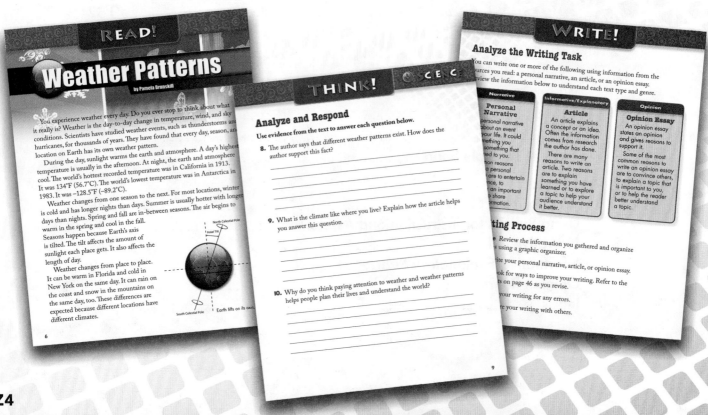

How It Works

Each unit in *I Read to Write* follows the same instructional plan and guides students to read, think, and write to multiple sources and across the curriculum.

Unit Content Areas

Science

Social Studies

Math

Unit Structure

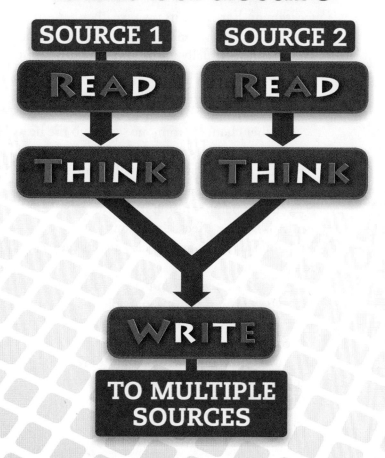

SOURCE 1   SOURCE 2

READ   READ

THINK   THINK

WRITE

TO MULTIPLE SOURCES

In **READ!**, students **closely read** high-interest **text sources** in three content areas, looking for key details and **citing evidence** from the text.

- Students practice **close reading** of **multiple complex texts** in each unit.

- **Engaging, colorful sources** align with new Lexile bands.

READ!

Weather Patterns

by Pamela Brunskill

You experience weather every day. Do you ever stop to think about what it really is? Weather is the day-to-day change in temperature, wind, and sky conditions. Scientists have studied weather events, such as thunderstorms and hurricanes, for thousands of years. They have found that every day, season, and location on Earth has its own weather pattern.

During the day, sunlight warms the earth and atmosphere. A day's highest temperature is usually in the afternoon. At night, the earth and atmosphere cool. The world's hottest recorded temperature was in California in 1913. It was 134°F (56.7°C). The world's lowest temperature was in Antarctica in 1983. It was −128.5°F (−89.2°C).

Weather changes from one season to the next. For most locations, winter is cold and has longer nights than days. Summer is usually hotter with longer days than nights. Spring and fall are in-between seasons. The air begins to warm in the spring and cool in the fall. Seasons happen because Earth's axis is tilted. The tilt affects the amount of sunlight each place gets. It also affects the length of day.

Weather changes from place to place. It can be warm in Florida and cold in New York on the same day. It can rain on the coast and snow in the mountains on the same day, too. These differences are expected because different locations have different climates.

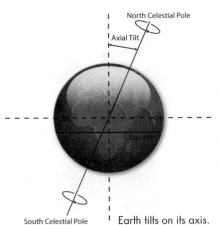

North Celestial Pole

Axial Tilt

Equator

South Celestial Pole

Earth tilts on its axis.

6

Cite Text Evidence

1. Determine Main Idea and Key Details What is the main idea of this article? Highlight a sentence that answers the question and label it 1. Write your answer below.

2. Quote Accurately Why are there seasonal weather patterns? Find the sentence that answers the question. Write the sentence below using quotation marks.

3. Use Text Features Why do scientists use weather maps? Highlight the text that answers the question and label it 3. Write your answer below.

Scientists use weather maps like this one to collect information about the weather and make predictions about weather patterns.

Climate is the average weather for a certain place over time. Usually, locations close to the equator have warmer climates. (The equator is an imaginary line around the center of Earth.) Locations closer to the North and South Poles have colder climates. Weather on the coast is cooler and moister than weather farther inland.

Scientists study weather and climate patterns. It helps them fore... helps them unders... the world. What a... like where you live...

● Students answer questions and **cite text evidence,** providing practice in an essential next generation assessment skill.

Preteach Vocabulary

Resources for preteaching key vocabulary from each article can be found at **irtw.zaner-bloser.com**.

ACADEMIC AND DOMAIN-SPECIFIC VOCABULARY

Included in the Teacher Edition are mini-lessons on academic and domain-specific vocabulary that provide students with word learning strategies to unlock the meaning of unfamiliar words and phrases.

OVERVIEW: THINK!

In **THINK!**, students answer **multiple-choice questions** to **check their comprehension** and then write answers to **constructed-response questions** that require a deeper analysis of the text.

● Evidence-based **selected response** questions require students to think beyond what is stated explicitly in the text.

THINK!

Weather Patterns
Check Comprehension

Choose the best answer for each question below.

4. How does the tilt of Earth's axis affect the changes in seasons?

  A It causes winter to be longer than summer in most places.

  B It makes the night longer the days nlight

rains next.

be

in

he

6. How are weather and climate different?

  A Weather changes every day. Climate is an average of weather in an area over time.

  B Weather is the hottest temperature recorded. Climate is the lowest temperature recorded.

  C Scientists can predict the climate, but they cannot predict weather.

  D Scientists use weather maps to learn about climate, not weather.

7. Which statement **best** explains why it can be warm in Florida and cold in New York on the same day?

  A New York is closer to the equator than Florida.

  B Florida is closer to the equator than New York.

  C Florida has more weather patterns than New York.

  D New York and Florida each have a coast.

SCIENCE

Analyze and Respond
Use evidence from the text to answer each question below.

8. The author says that different weather patterns exist. How does the author support this fact?

9. What is the climate like where you live? Explain how the article helps you answer this question.

10. Why do you think paying attention to weather and weather patterns helps people plan their lives and understand the world?

9

● Students practice supporting their responses with **evidence from the text** they read in the Read! section.

Z8

THINK!

A GARDEN JUST FOR YOU!

Choose the best answer for each question below.

Solve the Problem	Show Your Work

4. Sophia has $1.00. She decides to buy the beet seeds she needs. The seeds cost 10 cents each. How much money will she have left?

Ⓐ 9 cents

Ⓑ 10 cents

Ⓒ 81 cents

Ⓓ 90 cents

Use Sticky Note 1

5. Which statement about Sophia's garden plan is true?

Ⓐ Its area is 16 square feet.

Ⓑ Its perimeter is 8 feet.

Ⓒ The beets need 2 square feet.

Ⓓ The tomato needs 8 square feet.

Use Sticky Note 2

6. How much of the potting soil should be made up of compost?

Ⓐ $\frac{1}{2}$

Ⓑ $\frac{1}{3}$

Ⓒ $\frac{1}{4}$

Ⓓ $\frac{1}{5}$

Use Sticky Note 3

36

- In the Math unit, students **solve problems** using information they gathered from the text.

- Students are required to **explain their reasoning** in writing.

⊕ MATH

Analyze and Respond

Use evidence from the text to answer each question below.

7. Cole answered question 4 by choosing C, 81 cents. How do you think Cole got that answer? Is his answer correct? If not, explain how to do the problem so he understands how to get the correct answer.

_____

_____

_____

_____

8. How did you find the correct answer to question 5? Explain your reasoning.

_____

_____

_____

_____

_____

9. Sophia needs to mix 24 cubic feet of soil for ~~each type~~ much of explain

37

DIFFERENTIATED INSTRUCTION, COLLABORATION, AND ELL SUPPORT

The Teacher Edition includes differentiated instruction activities, ideas for promoting collaboration, and teaching tips for English language learners to engage students at all levels and provide practice with speaking and listening.

In **WRITE!**, students **respond to the sources** they read by synthesizing the information they learned from each source and producing writing that is grounded in **evidence from the texts**.

- Students have the flexibility to write in one or more of the text types:
  - **Narrative**
  - **Informative/ Explanatory**
  - **Opinion**

WRITE!

Analyze the Writing Task

You can write one or more of the following using information from the sources you read: a personal narrative, an article, or an opinion essay. Review the information below to understand each text type and genre.

Narrative	Informative/Explanatory	Opinion
Personal Narrative	**Article**	**Opinion Essay**
A personal narrative tells about an event from your life. It could be something you did or something that happened to you.	An article explains a concept or an idea. Often the information comes from research the author has done.	An opinion essay states an opinion and gives reasons to support it.
Common reasons to write a personal narrative are to entertain the audience, to remember an important event, or to share special information.	There are many reasons to write an article. Two reasons are to explain something you have learned or to explore a topic to help your audience understand it better.	Some of the most common reasons to write an opinion essay are to convince others, to explain a topic that is important to you, or to help the reader better understand a topic.

The Writing Process

1 **Prewrite** Review the information you gathered and organize your ideas using a graphic organizer.

2 **Draft** Write your personal narrative, article, or opinion essay.

3 **Revise** Look for ways to improve your writing. Refer to the writing traits on page 46 as you revise.

RUBRICS AND SIX TRAITS

In the back of the Teacher Edition are text-type-specific rubrics that break down the writing traits into six distinct point levels. These rubrics can be used for instructional purposes as students follow the writing process. They can also be used for assessment once students have completed their writing task.

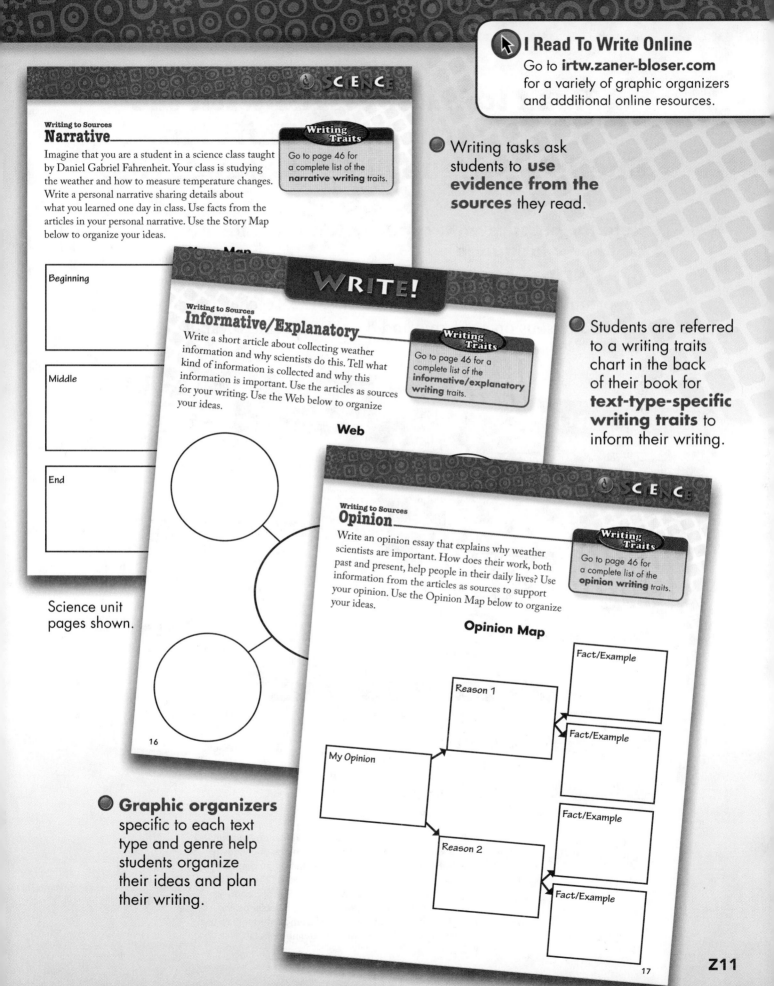

I Read To Write Online

Go to **irtw.zaner-bloser.com** for a variety of graphic organizers and additional online resources.

Writing to Sources
Narrative

Imagine that you are a student in a science class taught by Daniel Gabriel Fahrenheit. Your class is studying the weather and how to measure temperature changes. Write a personal narrative sharing details about what you learned one day in class. Use facts from the articles in your personal narrative. Use the Story Map below to organize your ideas.

Writing Traits
Go to page 46 for a complete list of the **narrative writing** traits.

Beginning

Middle

End

Science unit pages shown.

WRITE!

Writing to Sources
Informative/Explanatory

Write a short article about collecting weather information and why scientists do this. Tell what kind of information is collected and why this information is important. Use the articles as sources for your writing. Use the Web below to organize your ideas.

Writing Traits
Go to page 46 for a complete list of the **informative/explanatory writing** traits.

Web

16

Writing to Sources
Opinion

Write an opinion essay that explains why weather scientists are important. How does their work, both past and present, help people in their daily lives? Use information from the articles as sources to support your opinion. Use the Opinion Map below to organize your ideas.

Writing Traits
Go to page 46 for a complete list of the **opinion writing** traits.

Opinion Map

My Opinion

Reason 1

Fact/Example

Fact/Example

Reason 2

Fact/Example

Fact/Example

● Writing tasks ask students to **use evidence from the sources** they read.

● Students are referred to a writing traits chart in the back of their book for **text-type-specific writing traits** to inform their writing.

● **Graphic organizers** specific to each text type and genre help students organize their ideas and plan their writing.

17

Z11

I Read to Write aligns with the Key Instructional Shifts in English Language Arts Standards.

1 Regular practice with complex texts and their academic language

In **READ!**, students practice reading complex texts and have opportunities to grow their vocabularies. The Teacher Edition provides targeted lessons on academic and domain-specific vocabulary.

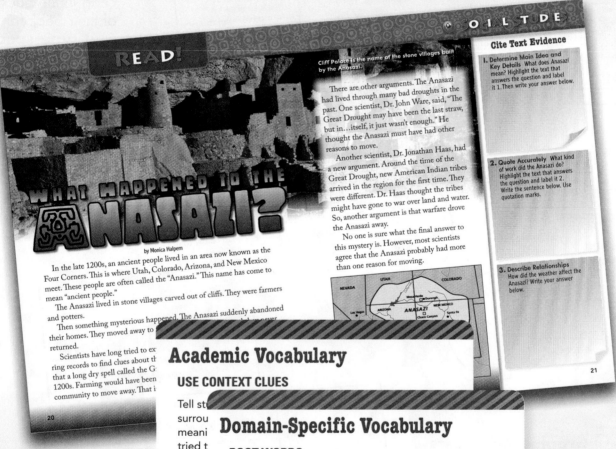

READ!

WHAT HAPPENED TO THE ANASAZI?

by Monica Halpern

In the late 1200s, an ancient people lived in an area now known as the Four Corners. This is where Utah, Colorado, Arizona, and New Mexico meet. These people are often called the "Anasazi." This name has come to mean "ancient people."

The Anasazi lived in stone villages carved out of cliffs. They were farmers and potters.

Then something mysterious happened. The Anasazi suddenly abandoned their homes. They moved away to [...] returned.

Scientists have long tried to ex[...] ring records to find clues about th[...] that a long dry spell called the G[...] 1200s. Farming would have been [...] community to move away. That i[...]

20

Cliff Palace is the name of the stone villages built by the Anasazi.

There are other arguments. The Anasazi had lived through many bad droughts in the past. One scientist, Dr. John Ware, said, "The Great Drought may have been the last straw, but in...itself, it just wasn't enough." He thought the Anasazi must have had other reasons to move.

Another scientist, Dr. Jonathan Haas, had a new argument. Around the time of the Great Drought, new American Indian tribes arrived in the region for the first time. They were different. Dr. Haas thought the tribes might have gone to war over land and water. So, another argument is that warfare drove the Anasazi away.

No one is sure what the final answer to this mystery is. However, most scientists agree that the Anasazi probably had more than one reason for moving.

Cite Text Evidence

1. **Determine Main Idea and Key Details** What does Anasazi mean? Highlight the text that answers the question and label it 1. Then write your answer below.

2. **Quote Accurately** What kind of work did the Anasazi do? Highlight the text that answers the question and label it 2. Write the sentence below. Use quotation marks.

3. **Describe Relationships** How did the weather affect the Anasazi? Write your answer below.

21

Academic Vocabulary

USE CONTEXT CLUES

Tell st[...]
surrou[...]
meani[...]
tried t[...]
Ask st[...]
the m[...]
have l[...]
of the[...]
by evi[...]

Domain-Specific Vocabulary

ROOT WORDS

Tell students that understanding the meanings of root words will help them unlock the meanings of unknown words. For example, the word *population* on page 24 includes the Latin root *pop*, which means "the people." The word *population* means "the number of people in a specific area." Write *population* and *popular* on the board, circle the root *pop*, and challenge students to use the meaning of the root word to define *popular*. (liked by many people)

2 Reading, writing, and speaking grounded in evidence from texts

In **THINK!**, students answer text-dependent questions and use evidence from the text to support their responses. In **WRITE!**, students use evidence from multiple sources to write within the Narrative, Informative/Explanatory, and Opinion text types.

THINK!

WHAT HAPPENED TO THE ANASAZI?

Check Comprehension

Choose the best answer for each question below.

4. Which statement **best** explains why the Great Drought was the "last straw" for the Anasazi?
   - A It forced the people to dig wells.
   - B It forced the people to grow less food.
   - C It forced the people to trade with other tribes.
   - D It forced the people to look for other places to grow food.

5. Which statement **best** explains how tree rings help scientists understand what might have happened to the Anasazi?
   - A They tell the age of trees.
   - B They tell what crops were grown.
   - C They provide clues as to how the people lived.
   - D They tell about the weather in an area over time.

6. How does the map help explain why the area where the Anasazi lived was called the Four Corners?
   - A It shows where two states meet.
   - B It shows that the area of the Anasazi's land was square.
   - C It shows where Utah, Colorado, Arizona, and New Mexico meet.
   - D It shows where four tribes lived.

7. Why would new tribes moving into the area cause the Anasazi to leave?
   - A There was not enough food to feed everyone.
   - B The tribes did not speak the same language.
   - C The tribes had different customs.
   - D The tribes fought over land and water.

22

SOCIAL STUDIES

Analyze and Respond

Use evidence from the text to answer each question below.

8. Some scientists argue that a great drought was not enough to make the Anasazi leave their homes. Why do these scientists think this way?

_____
_____
_____
_____

9. Some scientists argue that tribal warfare caused the Anasazi to leave. What are some reasons that the tribes may have gone to war?

_____
_____
_____
_____

10. The author says that no one really knows the answer to the Anasazi mystery. What have scientists done to try to solve the mystery?

_____
_____
_____
_____

23

WRITE!

Writing to Sources
Informative/Explanatory

The Anasazi and the people of New York City both lived in communities that experienced changes. Write a summary that compares the changes both communities experienced. Use facts and details from the sources in your writing. Use the Comparison Matrix below to help organize your ideas.

Writing Traits
Go to page 46 for a complete list of the informative/explanatory writing traits.

Comparison Matrix

Changes	Anasazi	People in New York City

30

3 Building knowledge through content-rich nonfiction

In each of *I Read to Write's* content area specific units, students increase their knowledge of the world around them by interacting with engaging nonfiction sources.

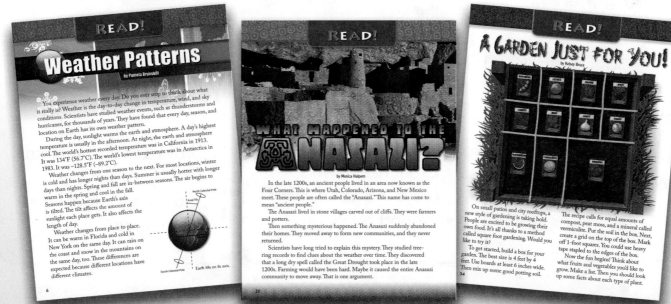

READ!
Weather Patterns
by Pamela Brunskill

You experience weather every day. Do you ever stop to think about what it really is? Weather is the day-to-day change in temperature, wind, and sky conditions. Scientists have studied weather events, such as thunderstorms and hurricanes, for thousands of years. They have found that every day, season, and location on Earth has its own weather pattern.

During the day, sunlight warms the earth and atmosphere. A day's highest temperature is usually in the afternoon. At night, the earth and atmosphere cool. The world's hottest recorded temperature was in California in 1913. It was 134°F (56.7°C). The world's lowest temperature was in Antarctica in 1983. It was −128.5°F (−89.2°C).

Weather changes from one season to the next. For most locations, winter is cold and has longer nights than days. Summer is usually hotter with longer days than nights. Spring and fall are in-between seasons. The air begins to warm in the spring and cool in the fall.

Seasons happen because Earth's axis is tilted. The tilt affects the amount of sunlight each place gets. It also affects the length of day.

Weather changes from place to place. It can be warm in Florida and cold in New York on the same day. It can rain on the coast and snow in the mountains on the same day, too. These differences are expected because different locations have different climates.

North Celestial Pole
Axial Tilt
South Celestial Pole
Earth tilts on its axis.

6

READ!
WHAT HAPPENED TO THE ANASAZI?
by Monica Halpern

In the late 1200s, an ancient people lived in an area now known as the Four Corners. This is where Utah, Colorado, Arizona, and New Mexico meet. These people are often called the "Anasazi." This name has come to mean "ancient people."

The Anasazi lived in stone villages carved out of cliffs. They were farmers and potters.

Then something mysterious happened. The Anasazi suddenly abandoned their homes. They moved away to form new communities, and they never returned.

Scientists have long tried to explain this mystery. They studied tree-ring records to find clues about the weather over time. They discovered that a long dry spell called the Great Drought took place in the late 1200s. Farming would have been hard. Maybe it caused the entire Anasazi community to move away. That is one argument.

20

READ!
A GARDEN JUST FOR YOU!
by Kelsey Bruce

On small patios and city rooftops, a new style of gardening is taking hold. People are excited to be growing their own food. It's all thanks to a method called square foot gardening. Would you like to try it?

To get started, build a box for your garden. The best size is 4 feet by 4 feet. Use boards at least 6 inches wide. Then mix up some good potting soil.

The recipe calls for equal amounts of compost, peat moss, and a mineral called vermiculite. Put the soil in the box. Next, create a grid on the top of the box. Mark off 1-foot squares. You could use heavy tape stapled to the edges of the box.

Now the fun begins! Think about what fruits and vegetables you'd like to grow. Make a list. Then you should look up some facts about each type of plant.

34

I Read to Write provides scaffolded instruction on the key skills and strategies students need for success on next generation assessments.

READ

Breaks down the close reading process students are expected to apply on next generation assessments

- Teaches students how to examine a text
- Guides students to interact with the text and identify key details

THINK

Deconstructs the types of text-dependent questions students will see on next generation assessments

- Teaches students to think beyond what is explicitly stated in the text
- Highlights critical thinking skills necessary for analyzing what the author had to say
- Examines how to use text evidence to support a response

WRITE

Guides students to analyze the types of writing tasks they will encounter on next generation assessments

- Breaks down the writing task and writing process
- Requires students to synthesize information from multiple sources
- Provides graphic organizers to help students plan their writing
- Reviews the writing traits specific to each text type and cues students to apply them to their writing

Zaner-Bloser Next Generation Assessment Practice simulates the online test-taking experience.

APPLY

These practice tests give students the opportunity to apply the skills and strategies they learned in *I Read to Write*. The tests include authentic, engaging text sources, as well as video sources. The sources are tied to a two-part writing performance task for each text type.

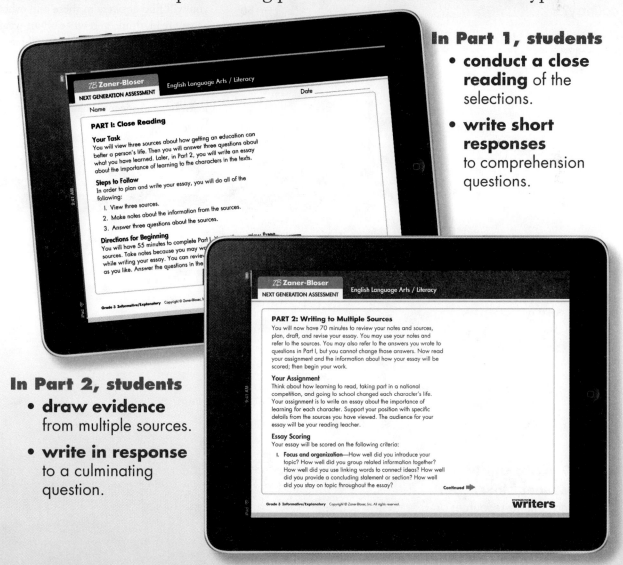

In Part 1, students
- **conduct a close reading** of the selections.
- **write short responses** to comprehension questions.

In Part 2, students
- **draw evidence** from multiple sources.
- **write in response** to a culminating question.

SCIENCE

Introduce the Unit

INTRODUCE THE THEME Ask a volunteer to read aloud the information about the unit theme at the bottom of page 4. Point out that, in this unit, students will have the opportunity to read, think, and respond in writing to the sources they read.

Use questions such as the following to guide students in a discussion about the theme:

- What do you know about weather in different parts of the country?

- How is a thermometer a useful tool?

Theme: Weather

Why is it usually warmer in Florida than it is in New York? Why do thermometers measure temperature in degrees Fahrenheit? In this unit, you will find answers to these and other questions as you read, think, and write about weather.

In "Weather Patterns," you will read about the changes in weather and climate around the globe and how scientists predict future weather.

In "Meet Daniel Gabriel Fahrenheit," you will learn how an inventor changed how we measure temperature.

4

I Read To Write Online
Go to **irtw.zaner-bloser.com** for additional online resources.

READ!

First, you will read an article and answer questions. These questions ask you to cite evidence from the text.

THINK!

Then, you will answer questions using information from the article, check your comprehension, and analyze what the author had to say.

WRITE!

Finally, it's time to write! You will use information from the sources you read to write one or more of the following: a personal narrative, an article, or an opinion essay. Each of these genres fits into a text type, as you can see below.

Narrative	Informative/ Explanatory	Opinion
Personal Narrative	**Article**	**Opinion Essay**
A **personal narrative** tells about an event from your life. It could be something you did or something that happened to you.	An **article** explains a concept or an idea. Often the information comes from research the author has done.	An **opinion essay** is a piece of writing that states an opinion and gives reasons to support it.

5

READ!

Tell students they will read each article twice: the first time to determine the main idea and the second time to take notes and cite evidence from the text.

THINK!

Explain that after they read each article, students will use information from the article to check their comprehension. They will also analyze what the author had to say, supporting their answers with evidence from the text.

WRITE!

Tell students they will use information from the sources they read to write one or more of the following: a narrative, an informative/explanatory piece, or an opinion piece. These writing tasks can be assigned or offered as student choice. Explain that they will use the writing process, which includes prewriting, drafting, revising, editing, and publishing. Use the chart on page 5 to introduce the text types and provide an overview of the genres.

READ!

Student Objectives

- Analyze a text source.
- Focus on academic vocabulary.
- Cite evidence from the text.

Close Reading Process

FIRST READING Ask students to read the article independently to understand the main idea. As they read, have students mark any words or ideas they find confusing. Ask them to share words or ideas they found confusing. Then discuss the main idea.

Note: You may wish to read the article aloud to students, pointing out key vocabulary words and discussing their meanings as you read. Students may also read with a partner.

SECOND READING Ask students to reread the text, citing information as indicated on the sticky notes on page 7. Tell students that this evidence will be important as they answer the text-dependent questions on pages 8–9.

Weather Patterns
by Pamela Brunskill

You experience weather every day. Do you ever stop to think about what it really is? Weather is the day-to-day change in temperature, wind, and sky conditions. Scientists have studied weather events, such as thunderstorms and hurricanes, for thousands of years. They have found that every day, season, and location on Earth has its own weather pattern. ①

During the day, sunlight warms the earth and atmosphere. A day's highest temperature is usually in the afternoon. At night, the earth and atmosphere cool. The world's hottest recorded temperature was in California in 1913. It was 134°F (56.7°C). The world's lowest temperature was in Antarctica in 1983. It was −128.5°F (−89.2°C).

Weather changes from one season to the next. For most locations, winter is cold and has longer nights than days. Summer is usually hotter with longer days than nights. Spring and fall are in-between seasons. The air begins to warm in the spring and cool in the fall. Seasons happen because Earth's axis is tilted. The tilt affects the amount of sunlight each place gets. It also affects the length of day.

Weather changes from place to place. It can be warm in Florida and cold in New York on the same day. It can rain on the coast and snow in the mountains on the same day, too. These differences are expected because different locations have different climates.

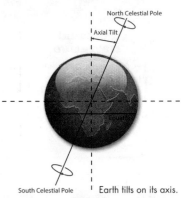

North Celestial Pole

Axial Tilt

Equator

South Celestial Pole   Earth tilts on its axis.

6

READ! Like a Writer

Use one or more of the following questions to guide discussion about the writing traits in the article:

Voice What makes the writer's voice sound confident and knowledgeable? Possible response: The writer sounds knowledgeable because she uses domain-specific vocabulary and includes a lot of facts.

Sentence Fluency What are some examples of sentences in the article that are informative and clear? Possible response: Sentences that include facts, such as *The world's hottest recorded temperature was in California in 1913* are informative.

Scientists use weather maps like this one to collect information about the weather and make predictions about weather patterns. ③

Climate is the average weather for a certain place over time. Usually, locations close to the equator have warmer climates. (The equator is an imaginary line around the center of Earth.) Locations closer to the North and South Poles have colder climates. Weather on the coast is cooler and moister than weather farther inland.

Scientists study weather and climate patterns. It helps them forecast, or predict, weather. It also helps them understand climate changes around the world. What are the weather and climate like where you live?

Cite Text Evidence

I. Determine Main Idea and Key Details What is the main idea of this article? Highlight a sentence that answers the question and label it 1. Write your answer below.

Weather patterns change by day, season, and location.

2. Quote Accurately Why are there seasonal weather patterns? Find the sentence that answers the question. Write the sentence below using quotation marks.

"Seasons happen because Earth's axis is tilted."

3. Use Text Features Why do scientists use weather maps? Highlight the text that answers the question and label it 3. Write your answer below.

They use information on weather maps to make predictions and understand weather patterns.

7

I. Determine Main Idea and Key Details Explain that the main idea is what the text is mostly about. Point out that the title provides a clue to the main idea (weather patterns) and that the author states the main idea in the first paragraph (weather patterns on Earth vary).

2. Quote Accurately Explain that it is important to use quotation marks when using a direct quotation, or the author's exact words. Tell students that quoting directly from a text is a good way to support a thought or an idea they have about the text.

3. Use Text Features Explain that authors use text features like captions to add information to the text. The information in the caption will help students answer the question about why scientists use weather maps.

Academic Vocabulary

PREFIXES AND SUFFIXES

Tell students that prefixes and suffixes are word parts that have their own meanings. Point out the word *highest* on page 6. Explain that *highest* includes the suffix *-est*, which means "most." *Highest* is used to describe the most high temperature. Now point out the word *inland* on page 7. This word includes the prefix *in-*, which means "toward." *Inland* means "going toward land." Explain that knowing the meanings of prefixes and suffixes can help readers define unfamiliar words.

Preteach Vocabulary

Resources for preteaching key vocabulary from this article can be found at **irtw.zaner-bloser.com**.

Student Objectives

- Check comprehension.
- Answer text-dependent questions.

Examine the Text

CHECK COMPREHENSION Tell students they will now answer questions based on the article they just read. Read the questions on page 8 aloud to students or have them read the questions independently. Discuss any words or ideas they find confusing. Encourage students to review the evidence they gathered on the sticky notes and revisit the text for additional details to help them answer the questions.

Weather Patterns

Check Comprehension

Choose the best answer for each question below.

4. How does the tilt of Earth's axis affect the changes in seasons?

   A It causes winter to be longer than summer in most places.

   B It makes the nights longer than the days during the spring.

   C It affects how long the days are and how much sunlight a place gets.

   D It affects how much it rains from one season to the next.

5. Which of the following can be called a weather pattern?

   A A weather event that happens again and again in the same location

   B The change in the seasons

   C Tornadoes occurring in the same area year after year

   D All of the above

6. How are weather and climate different?

   A Weather changes every day. Climate is an average of weather in an area over time.

   B Weather is the hottest temperature recorded. Climate is the lowest temperature recorded.

   C Scientists can predict the climate, but they cannot predict weather.

   D Scientists use weather maps to learn about climate, not weather.

7. Which statement **best** explains why it can be warm in Florida and cold in New York on the same day?

   A New York is closer to the equator than Florida.

   B Florida is closer to the equator than New York.

   C Florida has more weather patterns than New York.

   D New York and Florida each have a coast.

8

THINK! Like a Writer

Explain to students that the questions on pages 8 and 9 are designed to help them think about what the author had to say, what the author's purpose was, and what the structure of the text tells the reader.

Point out that the questions on page 9 ask them to support their answers with specific details from the text. Encourage students to ask themselves questions such as the following as they plan their responses:

- Where can I find details in the text that support my response?
- How do the images add to my understanding of the article?
- Can I add information from the article to make my response clearer?

Analyze and Respond

Possible responses appear below.

Use evidence from the text to answer each question below.

8. The author says that different weather patterns exist. How does the author support this fact?

The author supports this fact by explaining how seasons and temperatures change. They are different from place to place.

9. What is the climate like where you live? Explain how the article helps you answer this question.

Answers will vary but should demonstrate an understanding that climate is the average weather for a certain place over time. Students should explain that the article provides a definition of climate and examples of different climates.

10. Why do you think paying attention to weather and weather patterns helps people plan their lives and understand the world?

Since the weather can change every day, paying attention to the weather helps people decide what to wear each day and how to plan outdoor activities. Weather patterns help people know what to expect from the weather in different areas.

9

Use Evidence From the Text

ANALYZE AND RESPOND Tell students that they will now analyze what the author had to say. Read the questions on page 9 aloud to students or have them read the questions independently. Discuss any words or ideas they find confusing. Point out that they will need to include evidence from the text to support their responses.

AVOID PLAGIARISM: NOTE-TAKING STRATEGIES Ask students to explain what plagiarism is and why it should be avoided. To help students avoid plagiarism, encourage them to write down the main ideas from sources as they take notes instead of writing information from the text word for word. Suggest that they also use this strategy when filling in a graphic organizer during the prewriting step of the writing process.

After students have completed a graphic organizer in this unit, have partners review each other's graphic organizers and identify phrases or sentences that have been taken directly from the text. Encourage students to avoid using those phrases or sentences in their draft.

COLLABORATION

PEER TO PEER

Read aloud the questions on page 9. Ask students to think about their answers to each question individually. Then have students discuss their responses with a partner. Have students highlight details from the text to support their responses and agree upon an answer for each question. Then ask volunteers to share their responses with the class.

READ!

Student Objectives

- Analyze a text source.
- Focus on domain-specific vocabulary.
- Cite evidence from the text.

Close Reading Process

FIRST READING Ask students to read the article independently to understand the main idea. As they read, have students mark any words or ideas they find confusing. Ask them to share these words or ideas. Then discuss the main idea.

Note: You may wish to read the article aloud to students and discuss the meanings of the key vocabulary words. Students may also read with a partner.

SECOND READING Ask students to reread the text, highlighting information as indicated on the sticky notes on page 11. Tell students that this evidence will be important as they answer the text-dependent questions on pages 12–13.

Meet Daniel Gabriel Fahrenheit
Inventor of the First Standard Temperature Scale

by Kirsten W. Larson

Daniel Gabriel Fahrenheit was born in 1686. Growing up, he loved learning. He loved science. His family, however, were merchants. When his parents died suddenly in 1701, his life changed.

He wanted to study science, but his caretakers had another idea. They sent him to Holland to learn about business. However, when he was there, Fahrenheit became interested in scientific instruments. He wanted to learn about them, so he studied them.

Fahrenheit visited the men who made the instruments to learn more. During his travels, Fahrenheit met Ole Roemer. Roemer invented a new thermometer in 1708. It used alcohol inside a tube to measure temperature. When something he measured got warmer, the alcohol climbed up the tube.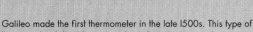

Fahrenheit studied Roemer's ideas. He thought he could make a better thermometer if he used mercury instead of alcohol. He thought mercury would be more sensitive to

Daniel Gabriel Fahrenheit

Galileo made the first thermometer in the late 1500s. This type of thermometer did not have a scale and was not accurate.

10

READ! Like a Writer

Use one or more of the following questions to guide discussion about the writing traits in the article:

Ideas What information does the author include to support the main idea that Fahrenheit invented a better thermometer? **Possible response: The author includes information that shows how Fahrenheit's thermometer was more accurate than Roemer's.**

Word Choice What precise words related to thermometers does the author use? **Possible response: The author uses the words *mercury, boiling and freezing points,* and *measuring scale* to help the reader understand thermometers.**

changes in heat and give a more accurate reading. Fahrenheit's theory was correct.

He made a measuring scale that was more detailed than Roemer's. It divided the boiling and freezing points of water. He worked hard on his thermometer. He tried different scales. Finally, in 1724, he created the thermometer that we have today. The boiling point of water, or 212 degrees, became the highest temperature on his scale. The freezing point was 32 degrees. People use this thermometer in many countries because it is so accurate.

Fahrenheit's work influenced others. People could now measure temperature changes from year to year. They could keep accurate records, and they could compare temperatures. Countries started weather stations to track temperature, rainfall, and other weather information. Today, scientists use these records to measure changes in Earth's weather patterns over time.

This is an early thermometer with both Fahrenheit's final scale (right) and Roemer's scale (left).

Cite Text Evidence

1. Quote Accurately What did Fahrenheit's caretakers want him to study? Find the sentence that answers this question. Write the sentence below using quotation marks.

"They sent him to Holland to learn about business."

2. Ask and Answer Questions How did Roemer's thermometer work? Highlight the text that answers the question and label it 2. Write your answer below.

It used alcohol to measure temperature. The alcohol climbed higher in the tube as the temperature got warmer.

3. Use Text Features Look at the pictures and captions in this article. When did Galileo make his thermometer? Write the answer and where you found it below.

Galileo made his first thermometer in the late 1500s. I found my answer in the caption on page 10.

11

1. Quote Accurately Explain to students that it is important to quote accurately from the text. Remind them to put quotation marks around any text they are using as a direct quotation.

2. Ask and Answer Questions Tell students that they should ask themselves questions about the ideas in a text as they read and then look for answers in the text. One question they might ask is, "How did Roemer's thermometer work?" Using this strategy helps readers better understand the text.

3. Use Text Features Remind students that a caption is the information or explanation that goes along with a picture. The images and captions in this article provide more background information about different types of thermometers and when they were invented.

Domain-Specific Vocabulary

ROOT WORDS

Tell students that a root is the basic part of a word that usually carries the meaning. Direct students to the word *thermometer* on page 10. Explain that this word includes two root words, *therm,* which means "heat," and *meter,* which means "measure." A thermometer is used to measure heat. Tell students that knowing the meanings of common root words can help them define unfamiliar words.

Preteach Vocabulary

Resources for preteaching key vocabulary from this article can be found at **irtw.zaner-bloser.com**.

THINK!

Student Objectives

- Check comprehension.
- Answer text-dependent questions.

Examine the Text

CHECK COMPREHENSION Tell students they will now answer questions based on the article they just read. Read the questions on page 12 aloud to students or have them read the questions independently. Discuss any words or ideas they find confusing. Encourage students to review the evidence they gathered on the sticky notes and revisit the text for additional details to help them answer the questions.

Meet Daniel Gabriel Fahrenheit
Check Comprehension

Choose the best answer for each question below.

4. How did Fahrenheit's temperature scale compare to Roemer's?

   (A) Fahrenheit's was more sensitive to changes in heat.
   (B) Fahrenheit's had more degree marks than Roemer's.
   (C) Fahrenheit's had fewer degree marks than Roemer's.
   (D) Fahrenheit's was less sensitive to cold.

5. Which statement **best** explains how Fahrenheit's work influenced others?

   (A) His work allowed scientists to measure the wind.
   (B) His work allowed scientists to measure water levels.
   (C) His work allowed scientists to accurately measure temperatures.
   (D) His work allowed scientists to measure the sun's heat.

6. Which statement **best** explains why people use Fahrenheit's thermometer?

   (A) It is filled with mercury.
   (B) It uses zero degrees as the lowest temperature.
   (C) It is accurate in its readings.
   (D) It uses 212 degrees as its highest temperature.

7. What role do weather stations play in measuring climate change?

   (A) Information they collect measures hot temperatures.
   (B) Information they collect measures cold temperatures.
   (C) Information they collect measures changes in weather patterns over a short time.
   (D) Information they collect measures changes in weather patterns over a long time.

12

THINK! Like a Writer

Explain to students that the questions on pages 12 and 13 are designed to help them think about what the author had to say, what the author's purpose was, and what the structure of the text tells the reader.

Point out that the questions on page 13 ask them to support their answers with specific details from the text. Encourage students to ask themselves questions such as the following as they plan their responses:

- Why did the author include images and captions?
- Can I add any information from the text to make my answer stronger?
- Where can I find details in the text to support my response?

Analyze and Respond

Possible responses appear below.

Use evidence from the text to answer each question below.

8. The author includes visuals of early thermometers with captions to describe them. How do these text features support the idea that Fahrenheit's thermometer was more successful than the other early thermometers?

   The photo on page 10 shows that Galileo's thermometer didn't have a scale, so it would be hard to read. Roemer's thermometer didn't have as many degrees, so it was not as accurate. Fahrenheit's thermometer, shown on page 11, was successful because it used mercury instead of alcohol. It was also more sensitive to changes in heat and therefore more accurate than previous thermometers.

9. The article includes details about Fahrenheit's childhood and education. Why did the author include these details?

   The author included these details so readers could see that Fahrenheit loved science when he was in school. This shows why he became a scientist.

10. Why is Fahrenheit an important scientist? Explain ways he influenced others.

    Fahrenheit's thermometer let people measure temperature changes from year to year and keep accurate records. It is because of his invention that countries all over the world can share information about temperature and weather. His invention helps scientists track weather and climate patterns.

13

Use Evidence From the Text

ANALYZE AND RESPOND Tell students that they will now analyze what the author had to say. Read the questions on page 13 aloud to students or have them read the questions independently. Discuss any words or ideas they find confusing. Point out that they will need to include evidence from the text to support their responses.

AVOID PLAGIARISM: PARAPHRASING Explain that plagiarism is using another person's words *as your own* and does not represent good writing. Tell students that one way to avoid plagiarism is by paraphrasing, or using your own words and sentence structures to explain a concept or idea. Use the following example to model paraphrasing:

> **Original:** He wanted to study science, but his caretakers had another idea.
>
> **Paraphrased:** He was most interested in science, but his caretakers thought he should study a different subject.

Have students work with partners to practice paraphrasing other sentences from the text.

ENGLISH LANGUAGE LEARNERS

Sentence Frames Students may need help answering the Analyze and Respond questions. Sentence frames can help give students who are unfamiliar with English a way to begin the answer to a question. Provide sentence frames like the ones below for students to use to answer the questions:

- The author states that ____.
- According to the text, ____.
- In my opinion, ____.

WRITE!

Student Objectives

- Analyze the writing task.
- Write to multiple sources.

Analyze the Writing Task

IDENTIFY PURPOSE AND AUDIENCE
Explain that all writing has a purpose and is aimed at a specific audience. Read and discuss with students the different options for their writing project, emphasizing the reasons or purposes for writing each genre and who the specific audience might be. Ask students to compare and contrast the purposes for writing each genre. Select a text type and genre for each student or invite them to read through the prompts on pages 15–16 and choose their own.

REVIEW THE WRITING PROCESS Read and discuss each of the steps in the writing process. Point out that these are the steps students will follow as they write. Ask them to identify key points to remember for each step.

Analyze the Writing Task

You can write one or more of the following using information from the sources you read: a personal narrative, an article, or an opinion essay. Review the information below to understand each text type and genre.

Narrative	Informative/Explanatory	Opinion
Personal Narrative A personal narrative tells about an event from your life. It could be something you did or something that happened to you. Common reasons to write a personal narrative are to entertain the audience, to remember an important event, or to share special information.	**Article** An article explains a concept or an idea. Often the information comes from research the author has done. There are many reasons to write an article. Two reasons are to explain something you have learned or to explore a topic to help your audience understand it better.	**Opinion Essay** An opinion essay states an opinion and gives reasons to support it. Some of the most common reasons to write an opinion essay are to convince others, to explain a topic that is important to you, or to help the reader better understand a topic.

The Writing Process

1 **Prewrite** Review the information you gathered and organize your ideas using a graphic organizer.

2 **Draft** Write your personal narrative, article, or opinion essay.

3 **Revise** Look for ways to improve your writing. Refer to the writing traits on page 46 as you revise.

4 **Edit** Check your writing for any errors.

5 **Publish** Share your writing with others.

14

Next Generation Assessment Practice

For additional practice with close reading and writing to multiple sources, use the **downloadable** Zaner-Bloser Next Generation Assessment Practice Tests. Modeled on the next generation assessments, the tests are designed to simulate an online test experience.

Writing to Sources
Narrative

Imagine that you are a student in a science class taught by Daniel Gabriel Fahrenheit. Your class is studying the weather and how to measure temperature changes. Write a personal narrative sharing details about what you learned one day in class. Use facts from the articles in your personal narrative. Use the Story Map below to organize your ideas.

Writing Traits

Go to page 46 for a complete list of the **narrative writing** traits.

Answers will vary.

Story Map

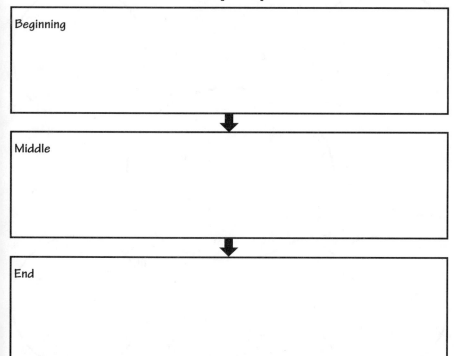

Beginning

Middle

End

15

Graphic Organizers

Additional graphic organizers can be found at **irtw.zaner-bloser.com**.

Use the Narrative Rubric

Go to Page T48

The **Narrative** text-type rubric can be used by students to plan and improve their writing. It can also be used to assess students' writing. Point out that this rubric emphasizes the use of **precise description, sensory details,** and **logical event sequence to tell a story**. You will find more information about the text-type rubrics on page T47.

Writing to Sources: Narrative

1 PREWRITE Tell students they will now use the information they learned and evidence gathered from each source to write a personal narrative about a day in science class. Use the following questions to guide discussion:

- What information can I use to describe the setting?

- What details would help develop the character(s)?

- What facts can I include to help the reader understand the causes and effects of weather and temperature changes?

Have students use the Story Map to organize their ideas.

2 DRAFT As students draft, remind them to keep their Story Map out and refer to it frequently.

3 REVISE Have students refer to the chart on page 46 for a complete list of the narrative writing traits. Remind them to ask questions such as the following as they revise:

- Did I engage my reader right from the beginning?

- Did I organize the events in a logical order?

4 EDIT Explain that during this step students should check their personal narrative for any errors in spelling, punctuation, capitalization, and grammar.

5 PUBLISH Remind students that neat presentation is important. Discuss how word-processing software can help them publish an attractive final copy (e.g., choosing a simple font, using the tab key to indent paragraphs).

WRITE!

Writing to Sources: Informative/Explanatory

1 **PREWRITE** Tell students they will now use the evidence they gathered to write an article about the importance of collecting weather information. Use the following questions to guide discussion:

- What is the main point I want to make?
- What details do I need to include to support my point?
- How can I order events logically in my article?

Have students use the Web to organize their ideas.

2 **DRAFT** As students draft, remind them to keep their Web out and refer to it frequently.

3 **REVISE** Have students refer to the chart on page 46 for a complete list of the informative/explanatory writing traits. Remind them to ask questions such as the following as they revise:

- Does my writing sound interesting and informative?
- What words can I use to be more specific and make my readers care about the topic?

4 **EDIT** Explain that during this step students should check their article for any errors in spelling, punctuation, capitalization, and grammar.

5 **PUBLISH** Remind students that neat presentation is important. Discuss how word-processing software can help them publish an attractive final copy (e.g., choosing a simple font, using the tab key to indent paragraphs).

T16

Writing to Sources
Informative/Explanatory

Write a short article about collecting weather information and why scientists do this. Tell what kind of information is collected and why this information is important. Use the articles as sources for your writing. Use the Web below to organize your ideas.

Writing Traits
Go to page 46 for a complete list of the **informative/explanatory writing** traits.

Web   Answers will vary.

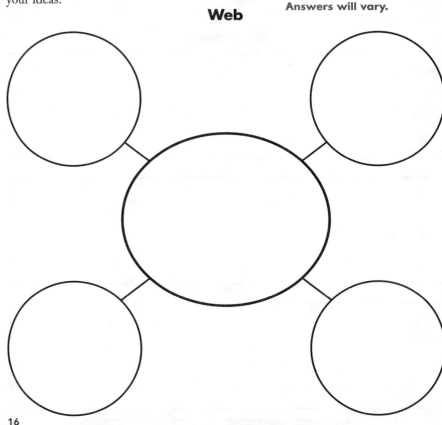

16

Use the Informative/Explanatory Rubric

Go to Page T49

The **Informative/Explanatory** text-type rubric can be used by students to plan and improve their writing. It can also be used to assess students' writing. Point out that this rubric emphasizes the importance of including a **strong introduction,** using an **engaging voice,** and providing **clear transitions** that connect ideas. You will find more information about the text-type rubrics on page T47.

Writing to Sources
Opinion

Write an opinion essay that explains why weather scientists are important. How does their work, both past and present, help people in their daily lives? Use information from the articles as sources to support your opinion. Use the Opinion Map below to organize your ideas.

Writing Traits

Go to page 46 for a complete list of the **opinion writing** traits.

Opinion Map

Answers will vary.

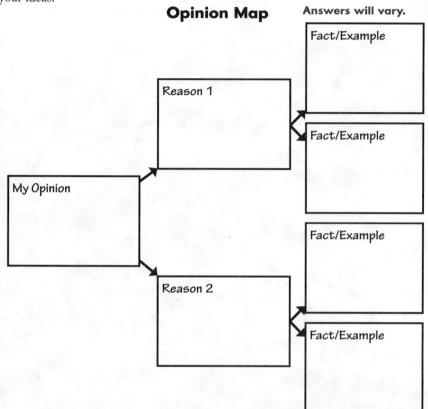

17

Use the Opinion Rubric

➤ Go to Page T50

The **Opinion** text-type rubric can be used by students to plan and improve their writing. It can also be used to assess students' writing. Point out that this rubric emphasizes the importance of clearly introducing and supporting a **point of view** with logically ordered **reasons** and **information**. You will find more information about the text-type rubrics on page T47.

Writing to Sources: Opinion

1 PREWRITE Tell students they will now use the evidence they gathered from each source to write an opinion essay about what weather scientists do and how their work helps people in their daily lives. Use the following questions to guide discussion:

- Are there any facts from the articles that I could use to strengthen my points?
- What details can I use to support my opinion?
- What examples can I add from my own life to support my ideas?

Have students use the Opinion Map to organize their ideas.

2 DRAFT As students draft, remind them to keep their Opinion Map out and refer to it frequently.

3 REVISE Have students refer to the chart on page 46 for a complete list of the opinion writing traits. Remind them to ask questions such as the following as they revise:

- Did I state my opinion clearly?
- Did I provide factual reasons to support my opinion?

4 EDIT Explain that during this step students should check their editorial for any errors in spelling, punctuation, capitalization, and grammar.

5 PUBLISH Remind students that neat presentation is important. Discuss how word-processing software can help them publish an attractive final copy (e.g., choosing a simple font, using the tab key to indent paragraphs).

SOCIAL STUDIES

Introduce the Unit

INTRODUCE THE THEME Ask a volunteer to read aloud the information about the unit theme at the top of page 18. Point out that, in this unit, students will have the opportunity to read, think, and respond in writing to the sources they read.

Use questions such as the following to guide students in a discussion about the theme:

- Why do you think a group of people would abandon or leave their community?

- What problems do you think a community might have when its population grows quickly?

 I Read To Write Online
Go to **irtw.zaner-bloser.com** for additional online resources.

Theme: Communities Throughout History

Could an entire community disappear? Has New York City always had a large population? In this unit, you will find answers to these and other questions as you read, think, and write about two different communities throughout history.

In "What Happened to the Anasazi?," you will read about the possible reasons why the ancient Anasazi people abandoned their homes.

In "A Changing New York City," you will learn about the city's humble beginnings and how things changed over time.

18

T18

READ!

First, you will read an article and answer questions. These questions ask you to cite evidence from the text.

THINK!

Then, you will answer questions using information from the article, check your comprehension, and analyze what the author had to say.

WRITE!

Finally, it's time to write! You will use information from the sources you read to write one or more of the following: a short story, a summary, or an opinion paper. Each of these genres fits into a text type, as you can see below.

Narrative	Informative/ Explanatory	Opinion
Short Story	**Summary**	**Opinion Paper**
A **short story** is a brief story that contains a plot, at least one character, and some conflict that needs to be resolved.	A **summary** is a short piece of writing that tells the most important points related to a larger topic.	An **opinion paper** is an essay that states an opinion and gives reasons to support it.

19

READ!

Tell students they will read each article twice: the first time to determine the main idea and the second time to take notes and cite evidence from the text.

THINK!

Explain that after they read each article, students will use information from the article to check their comprehension. They will also analyze what the author had to say, supporting their answers with evidence from the text.

WRITE!

Tell students they will use information from the sources they read to write one or more of the following: a narrative, an informative/explanatory piece, or an opinion piece. These writing tasks can be assigned or offered as student choice. Explain that they will use the writing process, which includes prewriting, drafting, revising, editing, and publishing. Use the chart on page 19 to introduce the text types and provide an overview of the genres.

Student Objectives

- Analyze a text source.
- Focus on academic vocabulary.
- Cite evidence from the text.

Close Reading Process

FIRST READING Ask students to read the article independently to understand the main idea. As they read, have students mark any words or ideas they find confusing. Ask them to share words or ideas they found confusing. Then discuss the main idea.

Note: You may wish to read the article aloud to students, pointing out key vocabulary words and discussing their meanings as you read. Students may also read with a partner.

SECOND READING Ask students to reread the text, citing evidence as indicated on the sticky notes on page 21. Tell students that this evidence will be important as they answer the text-dependent questions on pages 22–23.

READ!

WHAT HAPPENED TO THE ANASAZI?

by Monica Halpern

In the late 1200s, an ancient people lived in an area now known as the Four Corners. This is where Utah, Colorado, Arizona, and New Mexico meet. These people are often called the "Anasazi." This name has come to mean "ancient people." ①

The Anasazi lived in stone villages carved out of cliffs. They were farmers and potters. ②

Then something mysterious happened. The Anasazi suddenly abandoned their homes. They moved away to form new communities, and they never returned.

Scientists have long tried to explain this mystery. They studied tree-ring records to find clues about the weather over time. They discovered that a long dry spell called the Great Drought took place in the late 1200s. Farming would have been hard. Maybe it caused the entire Anasazi community to move away. That is one argument.

20

READ! Like a Writer

Use one or more of the following questions to guide discussion about the writing traits in the article:

Ideas How does the author stay focused on the topic? **Possible response: The author gives information only about the Anasazi and what might have happened to them.**

Organization What makes the paragraphs in this article well organized? **Possible response: Each paragraph sticks to one main idea.**

Cliff Palace is the name of the stone villages built by the Anasazi.

There are other arguments. The Anasazi had lived through many bad droughts in the past. One scientist, Dr. John Ware, said, "The Great Drought may have been the last straw, but in…itself, it just wasn't enough." He thought the Anasazi must have had other reasons to move.

Another scientist, Dr. Jonathan Haas, had a new argument. Around the time of the Great Drought, new American Indian tribes arrived in the region for the first time. They were different. Dr. Haas thought the tribes might have gone to war over land and water. So, another argument is that warfare drove the Anasazi away.

No one is sure what the final answer to this mystery is. However, most scientists agree that the Anasazi probably had more than one reason for moving.

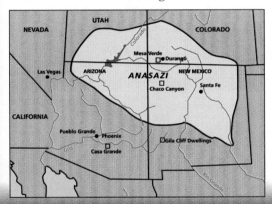

Cite Text Evidence

1. Determine Main Idea and Key Details What does *Anasazi* mean? Highlight the text that answers the question and label it 1. Then write your answer below.

Anasazi means "ancient people."

2. Quote Accurately What kind of work did the Anasazi do? Highlight the text that answers the question and label it 2. Write the sentence below. Use quotation marks.

"They were farmers and potters."

3. Describe Relationships How did the weather affect the Anasazi? Write your answer below.

The lack of rain made it difficult for the Anasazi to grow crops.

21

1. Determine Main Idea and Key Details Tell students that writers use details and examples to develop a topic. Explain that the meaning of "Anasazi" is a key detail that helps the reader understand who the Anasazi were.

2. Quote Accurately Remind students that it is important to use quotation marks when using a direct quotation, or the author's exact words. Tell students that quoting directly from a text is a good way to support a thought or an idea they have about the text.

3. Describe Relationships Tell students that describing relationships in a text includes explaining causes and effects. In this article, one cause-effect relationship is that the Great Drought may have caused the Anasazi to move because it was difficult to grow crops.

Academic Vocabulary

USE CONTEXT CLUES

Tell students they can use context, or the words surrounding an unfamiliar word, to unlock that word's meaning. Point out the sentences *Scientists have long tried to explain this mystery.* and *That was one argument.* Ask students which words in the sentences are clues to the meaning of *argument*. Help them see that the phrase *have long tried to explain* provides a clue to the meaning of the word *argument*: an explanation that is supported by evidence.

Preteach Vocabulary

Resources for preteaching key vocabulary from this article can be found at **irtw.zaner-bloser.com**.

Student Objectives

- Check comprehension.
- Answer text-dependent questions.

Examine the Text

CHECK COMPREHENSION Tell students they will now answer questions based on the article they just read. Read the questions on page 22 aloud to students or have them read the questions independently. Discuss any words or ideas they find confusing. Encourage students to review the evidence they gathered on the sticky notes and revisit the text for additional details to help them answer the questions.

WHAT HAPPENED TO THE ANASAZI?

Check Comprehension

Choose the best answer for each question below.

4. Which statement **best** explains why the Great Drought was the "last straw" for the Anasazi?

Ⓐ It forced the people to dig wells.

Ⓑ It forced the people to grow less food.

Ⓒ It forced the people to trade with other tribes.

Ⓓ It forced the people to look for other places to grow food.

5. Which statement **best** explains how tree rings help scientists understand what might have happened to the Anasazi?

Ⓐ They tell the age of trees.

Ⓑ They tell what crops were grown.

Ⓒ They provide clues as to how the people lived.

Ⓓ They tell about the weather in an area over time.

6. How does the map help explain why the area where the Anasazi lived was called the Four Corners?

Ⓐ It shows where two states meet.

Ⓑ It shows that the area of the Anasazi's land was square.

Ⓒ It shows where Utah, Colorado, Arizona, and New Mexico meet.

Ⓓ It shows where four tribes lived.

7. Why would new tribes moving into the area cause the Anasazi to leave?

Ⓐ There was not enough food to feed everyone.

Ⓑ The tribes did not speak the same language.

Ⓒ The tribes had different customs.

Ⓓ The tribes fought over land and water.

22

THINK! Like a Writer

Explain to students that the questions on pages 22 and 23 are designed to help them think about what the author had to say, what the author's purpose was, and what the structure of the text tells the reader.

Point out that the questions on page 23 ask them to support their answers with specific details from the text. Encourage students to ask themselves questions such as the following as they plan their responses:

- Where can I find details in the text that support my response?
- What did the author say that makes me think that?
- Can I add any information from the text to make my response stronger?

Analyze and Respond

Possible responses appear below.

Use evidence from the text to answer each question below.

8. Some scientists argue that a great drought was not enough to make the Anasazi leave their homes. Why do these scientists think this way?

The scientists know from the study of the tree rings that the Anasazi had lived through bad droughts in the past. The scientists think that something else must have caused the Anasazi to move.

9. Some scientists argue that tribal warfare caused the Anasazi to leave. What are some reasons that the tribes may have gone to war?

The author states, "Dr. Haas thought the tribes might have gone to war over land and water." People need land and water to live, so the tribes must have fought over how much land and water each tribe needed.

10. The author says that no one really knows the answer to the Anasazi mystery. What have scientists done to try to solve the mystery?

Scientists studied the tree rings to see what the weather was like during the time that the Anasazi were in the area. They found that there were droughts that would have caused the crops to fail. Evidence has also been found that new American Indian tribes moved into the area and may have caused the Anasazi to leave.

23

Use Evidence From the Text

ANALYZE AND RESPOND Tell students that they will now analyze what the author had to say. Read the questions on page 23 aloud to students or have them read the questions independently. Discuss any words or ideas they find confusing. Point out that they will need to include evidence from the text to support their responses.

AVOID PLAGIARISM: PARAPHRASING Explain that plagiarism is using another person's words *as your own* and does not represent good writing. Tell students that one way to avoid plagiarism is by paraphrasing, or using your own words and sentence structures to explain a concept or idea. Use the following example to model paraphrasing:

> **Original:** The Anasazi suddenly abandoned their homes. They moved away to form new communities, and they never returned.

> **Paraphrased:** The Anasazi left and never came back. They started new communities someplace else.

Have students work with partners to practice paraphrasing.

DIFFERENTIATED INSTRUCTION

REINFORCEMENT

Break Down the Questions Read aloud the questions on page 23. Ask students to explain in their own words what each question is asking. If needed, guide them in restating the question. Have students discuss what it means to use evidence to support their answers. Ask them to point out some details from the article that might be useful for answering one or more of the questions. Encourage students to use this strategy whenever they are asked to write an evidence-based response.

READ!

Student Objectives

- Analyze a text source.
- Focus on domain-specific vocabulary.
- Cite evidence from the text.

Close Reading Process

FIRST READING Ask students to read the article independently to understand the main idea. As they read, have students mark any words or ideas they find confusing. Ask them to share these words or ideas. Then discuss the main idea.

Note: You may wish to read the article aloud to students, pointing out key vocabulary words and discussing their meanings as you read. Students may also read with a partner.

SECOND READING Ask students to reread the text, citing evidence as indicated on the sticky notes on page 25. Tell students that this evidence will be important as they answer the text-dependent questions on pages 26–27.

A Changing New York City

by Marie Halpern

New York, 1600s

Today, New York City is the largest city in the United States. More than 8 million people live there. Tall skyscrapers line its streets and crowds of people hurry from place to place.

New York City didn't always look like this. The Dutch were the first people to build a town on Manhattan Island in ① 1625. They called it New Amsterdam after their capital in Holland. The population was about 1,000 by 1656.

The British took over the town and renamed it New York in 1664. The town grew. By 1700 the population was about 5,000.

New York City was still a small country town. There were only a few hundred houses made of brick or wood in the town. Most people farmed and hunted for food in the woods nearby. Goats, sheep, pigs, and cattle wandered the muddy streets. People walked everywhere.

New York, 1800s

The city continued to grow and prosper. Large numbers of immigrants arrived from Europe, Asia, and Latin America in the late 1800s. They were looking for jobs and a better life. Many had few skills. Some worked as builders. Others worked in factories.

Most immigrants had little money. They usually lived in crowded neighborhoods. They were packed into six-story, walk-up buildings called tenements. A single tenement might house 300 people in its 84 rooms.

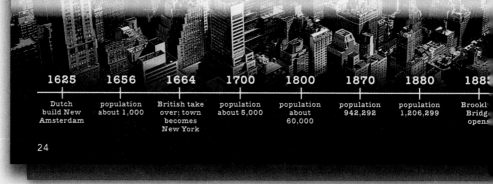

1625	1656	1664	1700	1800	1870	1880	188
Dutch build New Amsterdam	population about 1,000	British take over; town becomes New York	population about 5,000	population about 60,000	population 942,292	population 1,206,299	Brookl Bridg opens

24

READ! Like a Writer

Use one or more of the following questions to guide discussion about the writing traits in the article:

Voice Is the writer's voice formal or casual? How is this appropriate for the writer's purpose? **Possible response: The writer's voice is formal, which is appropriate for an informative piece.**

Sentence Fluency What makes the sentences in this article clear and direct? **Possible response: The sentences are well written and not wordy.**

Families often worked together in their crowded apartments.

New inventions changed the city. Electric streetcars carried workers to their jobs. Electric streetlights made the streets brighter and safer. So, more people went out in the evenings to classes or for fun.

Then in 1883, the Brooklyn Bridge opened. It was the first steel suspension bridge. It connected Brooklyn and ② Manhattan, separate cities at the time. Just fifteen years later, the city of Brooklyn became part of New York City.

By 1900 New York City's population was nearly 3.5 million. About 1.3 million were immigrants, who helped build New York City.

1886	1890	1898	1900	2013
...ance gives ...e United ...tates the Statue of Liberty.	population 1,515,301	Brooklyn and Manhattan become one city	population 3,437,202	population 8,405,837

Cite Text Evidence

1. Determine Main Idea and Key Details Who founded New Amsterdam? Highlight the text that answers the question and label it 1. Then write your answer below.

> **The Dutch founded New Amsterdam.**

2. Describe Relationships Highlight the answers to the questions below and label them 2. Write your answers below the questions.

- What kind of bridge is the Brooklyn Bridge?
  It is a steel suspension bridge.

- How did the Brooklyn Bridge affect New York City?
  It connected Brooklyn and Manhattan. Because of that, Brooklyn became part of New York City.

3. Use Text Features Write your answers below the questions.

- What was the population of New York City in 1900?
  3,437,202

- What was the population in 2013?
  8,405,837

- Where did you find your answers?
  I found my answers on the timeline.

25

1. Determine Main Idea and Key Details Explain that authors include key details to support the main ideas in a text. Tell students that the highlighted sentences provide key details about the people who first lived in what is now New York City.

2. Describe Relationships Remind students that describing relationships in a text includes explaining causes and effects. One important cause-effect relationship in this article is how the Brooklyn Bridge changed New York City.

3. Use Text Features Remind students that authors include text features, such as graphs, charts, or timelines, to give readers more information in a different form. Tell students that this information is as important as the main text.

Domain-Specific Vocabulary

ROOT WORDS

Tell students that understanding the meanings of root words will help them unlock the meanings of unknown words. For example, the word *population* on page 24 includes the Latin root *pop*, which means "the people." The word *population* means "the number of people in a specific area." Write *population* and *popular* on the board, circle the root *pop*, and challenge students to use the meaning of the root word to define *popular*. (liked by many people)

Preteach Vocabulary

Resources for preteaching key vocabulary from this article can be found at **irtw.zaner-bloser.com**.

Student Objectives

- Check comprehension.
- Answer text-dependent questions.

Examine the Text

CHECK COMPREHENSION Tell students they will now answer questions based on the article they just read. Read the questions on page 26 aloud to students or have them read the questions independently. Discuss any words or ideas they find confusing. Encourage students to review the evidence they gathered on the sticky notes and revisit the text for additional details to help them answer the questions.

A Changing New York City
Check Comprehension

Choose the best answer for each question below.

4. The Brooklyn Bridge opened in 1883. What conclusion can be drawn about why this was an important event?
   - Ⓐ It was made of steel.
   - **Ⓑ** It made travel easier between New York City and Brooklyn.
   - Ⓒ It caused people to stop using electric streetcars.
   - Ⓓ It hurt business in New York City.

5. How did streetlights affect New York City?
   - Ⓐ They created more jobs.
   - Ⓑ They made the city more beautiful.
   - **Ⓒ** They allowed people to go out at night.
   - Ⓓ They created more restaurants.

6. Which statement **best** supports the reason why so many people lived in the crowded tenements?
   - Ⓐ They didn't want to live alone.
   - Ⓑ They didn't need much space.
   - Ⓒ They could afford better places.
   - **Ⓓ** They did not have enough money to live elsewhere.

7. Which statement **best** supports the reason why immigrants worked as builders and in factories?
   - Ⓐ They had good educations.
   - Ⓑ They were paid well for their work.
   - **Ⓒ** They had few skills and little education.
   - Ⓓ They had done those jobs before.

26

THINK! Like a Writer

Explain to students that the questions on pages 26 and 27 are designed to help them think about what the author had to say, what the author's purpose was, and what the structure of the text tells the reader.

Point out that the questions on page 26 ask them to support their answers with specific details from the text. Encourage students to ask themselves

questions such as the following as they plan their responses:

- Where can I find key details in the text to support my response?
- What information did the author include that can help me predict how New York City might change in the future?
- What information from the text can make my response stronger?

Analyze and Respond

Possible responses appear below.

Use evidence from the text to answer each question below.

8. The author says that immigrants came to New York City from many different countries. Explain why you think the immigrants chose to come to New York City.

Immigrants from Europe, Asia, and Latin America came to New York City to try to improve their lives. They came to find jobs that were not available in their home country.

9. List three ways that New York City changed over time. How might it continue to change?

More people moved to New York. New businesses and places to eat opened. Electric lights and streetcars made it easier to get around the city and to stay out later at night. The area of the city got bigger when smaller cities around New York became part of the city. I think more people will continue to move to the city and taller buildings will continue to be built.

10. The timeline shows how New York City's population grew over time. Explain why the population grew larger.

The population grew over time because immigrants kept coming to the city to find work and a better life. The population also grew when Brooklyn became part of the city after the Brooklyn Bridge was built.

27

Use Evidence From the Text

ANALYZE AND RESPOND Tell students that they will now analyze what the author had to say. Read the questions on page 27 aloud to students or have them read the questions independently. Discuss any words or ideas they find confusing. Point out that they will need to include evidence from the text to support their responses.

AVOID PLAGIARISM: QUOTING ACCURATELY Remind students that plagiarism is using another person's words *as your own* and does not represent good writing. Tell them that one way to avoid plagiarism is to quote accurately. To do this, students should include a speaker tag, such as *The author states*, copy the original text carefully, and use quotation marks around the text. Share this example with students:

Original: It was the first steel suspension bridge.

Quotation: The author states, "It was the first steel suspension bridge."

Have students work with partners to practice quoting accurately from the text.

COLLABORATION
PEER GROUPS

Have students form small groups. Ask them to take turns reading aloud their responses to the questions on page 27. Have students identify the evidence group members used to support their responses. Invite them to suggest additional evidence that would make one another's responses stronger. Encourage students to revise their answers based on the discussion.

WRITE!

Student Objectives

- Analyze the writing task.
- Write to multiple sources.

Analyze the Writing Task

IDENTIFY PURPOSE AND AUDIENCE
Explain that all writing has a purpose and is aimed at a specific audience. Read and discuss with students the different options for their writing project, emphasizing the reasons or purposes for writing each genre and who the specific audience might be. Ask students to compare and contrast the purposes for writing within each genre. Select a text type and genre for each student or invite them to read through the prompts on pages 29–31 and choose their own.

REVIEW THE WRITING PROCESS Read and discuss each of the steps in the writing process. Point out that these are the steps students will follow as they write. Ask them to identify key points to remember for each step.

WRITE!

Analyze the Writing Task

You can write one or more of the following using information from the sources you read: a short story, a summary, or an opinion paper. Review the information below to understand each text type and genre.

Narrative	Informative/Explanatory	Opinion
Short Story	**Summary**	**Opinion Paper**
A short story is a brief story that contains a plot, at least one character, and some conflict that needs to be resolved. The most common reasons to write a short story are to be creative and to entertain.	A summary is a short piece of writing that tells the most important points in a longer piece of writing. Writing a summary can help you understand a topic and explain the most important information to your audience.	An opinion paper is an essay that states an opinion and gives reasons to support it. Some of the most common reasons to write an opinion paper are to convince others, to explain a topic that is important to you, and to help the reader better understand a topic.

The Writing Process

1 Prewrite Review the information you gathered and organize your ideas using a graphic organizer.

2 Draft Write your short story, summary, or opinion paper.

3 Revise Look for ways to improve your writing. Refer to the writing traits on page 46 as you revise.

4 Edit Check your writing for any errors.

5 Publish Share your writing with others.

28

Next Generation Assessment Practice

PDF For additional practice with close reading and writing to multiple sources, use the **downloadable** Zaner-Bloser Next Generation Assessment Practice Tests. Modeled on the next generation assessments, the tests are designed to simulate an online test experience.

Writing to Sources
Narrative

Write a short story about an Anasazi person meeting a new immigrant to New York City. Explain what advice they could give each other on how to adapt to the changes they are experiencing. Use facts and details from the sources in your writing. Use the Venn Diagram below to help organize your ideas.

Writing Traits

Go to page 46 for a complete list of the **narrative writing** traits.

Answers will vary.

Venn Diagram

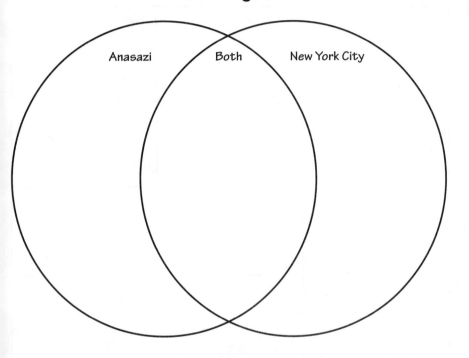

Anasazi   Both   New York City

29

Graphic Organizers

Additional graphic organizers can be found at **irtw.zaner-bloser.com**.

Use the Narrative Rubric

➤ Go to Page T48

The **Narrative** text-type rubric can be used by students to plan and improve their writing. It can also be used to assess students' writing. Point out that this rubric emphasizes the use of **precise description, sensory details,** and **logical event sequence to tell a story**. You will find more information about the text-type rubrics on page T47.

Writing to Sources: Narrative

1 PREWRITE Tell students they will now use the information they learned from each source to write a short story about people from different communities meeting. Use the following questions to guide discussion:

- Which details can I use to describe the events in my story?
- What details would help describe the character(s)?
- What facts can I add to interest my reader?

Have students use the Venn Diagram to organize their ideas.

2 DRAFT As students draft, remind them to keep their Venn Diagram out and refer to it frequently.

3 REVISE Have students refer to the chart on page 46 for a complete list of the narrative writing traits. Remind them to ask questions such as the following as they revise:

- Did I include words and phrases that help the reader "see" the characters?
- Did I use different sentence beginnings?

4 EDIT Explain that during this step students should check their short story for any errors in spelling, punctuation, capitalization, and grammar.

5 PUBLISH Remind students that neat presentation is important. Discuss how word-processing software can help them publish an attractive final copy (e.g., choosing a simple font, using the tab key to indent paragraphs).

WRITE!

Writing to Sources: Informative/Explanatory

1 PREWRITE Tell students they will now use the evidence they gathered from each source to write a summary about how two communities changed over time. Use the following questions to guide discussion:

- What important ideas do I want to support in my summary?

- What information and details will add to the reader's knowledge about how these communities changed?

- How can I organize my summary in a logical way?

Have students use the Comparison Matrix to organize their ideas.

2 DRAFT As students draft, remind them to keep their Comparison Matrix out and refer to it frequently.

3 REVISE Have students refer to the chart on page 46 for a complete list of the informative/explanatory writing traits. Remind them to ask questions such as the following as they revise:

- Did I state the important points clearly?

- Did I support the important points with facts and evidence?

4 EDIT Explain that during this step, students should check their summary for any errors in spelling, punctuation, capitalization, and grammar.

5 PUBLISH Remind students that neat presentation is important. Discuss how word-processing software can help them publish an attractive final copy (e.g., choosing a simple font).

T30

Writing to Sources

Informative/Explanatory

The Anasazi and the people of New York City both lived in communities that experienced changes. Write a summary that compares the changes both communities experienced. Use facts and details from the sources in your writing. Use the Comparison Matrix below to help organize your ideas.

Writing Traits

Go to page 46 for a complete list of the **informative/explanatory writing** traits.

Comparison Matrix   Answers will vary.

Changes	Anasazi	People in New York City

30

Use the Informative/Explanatory Rubric

➤Go to Page T49

The **Informative/Explanatory** text-type rubric can be used by students to plan and improve their writing. It can also be used to assess students' writing. Point out that this rubric emphasizes the importance of including a **strong introduction,** using an **engaging voice,** and providing **clear transitions** that connect ideas. You will find more information about the text-type rubrics on page T47.

Writing to Sources
Opinion

The Anasazi decided to leave their land, while the people in New York City stayed. Write an opinion paper on what you think about both decisions. Do you agree with their decisions? Use evidence from the sources to support your opinion. Use the Concept Map below to help organize your ideas.

Writing Traits

Go to page 46 for a complete list of the **opinion writing** traits.

Answers will vary.

Concept Map

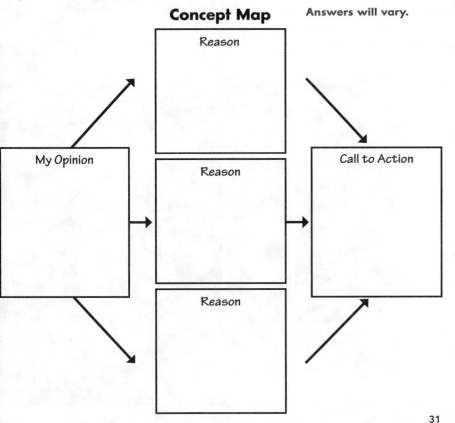

My Opinion

Reason

Reason

Reason

Call to Action

31

Use the Opinion Rubric

➤ Go to Page T50

The **Opinion** text-type rubric can be used by students to plan and improve their writing. It can also be used to assess students' writing. Point out that this rubric emphasizes the importance of clearly introducing and supporting a **point of view** with logically ordered **reasons** and **information**. You will find more information about the text-type rubrics on page T47.

Writing to Sources: Opinion

1 PREWRITE Tell students they will now use the evidence they gathered to write an opinion paper about the decisions the Anasazi people and the people in New York City made. Use the following questions to guide discussion:

- How can I clearly state my opinion about the communities?

- Which facts and details will support my opinion?

- How can I use a convincing voice?

Have students use the Concept Map to organize their ideas.

2 DRAFT As students draft, remind them to keep their Concept Map out and refer to it frequently.

3 REVISE Have students refer to the chart on page 46 for a complete list of the narrative writing traits. Remind them to ask questions such as the following as they revise:

- Did I choose precise words and fair language to support my opinion?

- Did I use a variety of sentence lengths?

4 EDIT Explain that during this step students should check their opinion paper for any errors in spelling, punctuation, capitalization, and grammar.

5 PUBLISH Remind students that neat presentation is important. Discuss how word-processing software can help them publish an attractive final copy (e.g., choosing a simple font, using the tab key to indent paragraphs).

Introduce the Unit

INTRODUCE THE THEME Ask a volunteer to read aloud the information about the unit theme at the top of page 32. Point out that, in this unit, students will have the opportunity to read, think, and respond in writing to the sources they read.

Use questions such as the following to guide students in a discussion about the theme:

- What do you know about plants?

- What parts of a tree can you name?

- Have you ever planted a garden? What steps were involved?

I Read To Write Online
Go to **irtw.zaner-bloser.com** for additional online resources.

T32

 MATH

Theme: Plants

What is the biggest tree in the world? Can people really grow food on a city rooftop? In this unit, you will find answers to these and other questions as you read, think, and write about plants.

In "A Garden Just for You!," you will learn how to plant your own square foot garden.

In "What a Tree!," you will read about General Sherman, a giant sequoia tree that is one of the largest living things on Earth.

32

READ!

First, you will read an article and answer questions. These questions ask you to cite evidence from the text.

THINK!

Then, you will answer questions using information from the article, solve math problems, and explain your thinking.

WRITE!

Finally, it's time to write! You will use information from the sources you read to write one or more of the following: a short story, a compare-and-contrast essay, or an editorial. Each of these genres fits into a text type, as you can see below.

Narrative	Informative/Explanatory	Opinion
Short Story A **short story** is a brief story that has a full plot, at least one character, and a problem that is solved.	**Compare-and-Contrast Essay** A **compare-and-contrast essay** tells how two or more things are alike and different.	**Editorial** An **editorial** is a piece of writing, often published in a newspaper, that tells the author's opinion.

33

READ!

Tell students they will read each article twice: the first time to determine the main idea and the second time to take notes and cite evidence from the text.

THINK!

Explain that after they read each article, students will use information from the article to solve math problems. They will also answer questions and explain their reasoning.

WRITE!

Tell students they will use information from the sources they read to write one or more of the following: a narrative, an informative/explanatory piece, or an opinion piece. These writing tasks can be assigned or offered as student choice. Explain that they will use the writing process, which includes prewriting, drafting, revising, editing, and publishing. Use the chart on page 33 to introduce the text types and provide an overview of the genres.

READ!

Student Objectives

- Analyze a text source.
- Focus on academic vocabulary.
- Cite evidence from the text.

Close Reading Process

FIRST READING Ask students to read the article independently to understand the main idea. As they read, have students mark any words or ideas they find confusing. Ask them to share words or ideas they found confusing. Then discuss the main idea.

Note: You may wish to read the article aloud to students, pointing out key vocabulary words and discussing their meanings as you read. Students may also read with a partner.

SECOND READING Ask students to reread the text, citing evidence as indicated on the sticky notes on page 35. Tell students that this evidence will be important as they solve the problems on pages 36–37.

A GARDEN JUST FOR YOU!

by Kelsey Bruce

On small patios and city rooftops, a new style of gardening is taking hold. People are excited to be growing their own food. It's all thanks to a method called square foot gardening. Would you like to try it?

To get started, build a box for your garden. The best size is 4 feet by 4 feet. Use boards at least 6 inches wide. Then mix up some good potting soil.

34

The recipe calls for equal amounts of ③ compost, peat moss, and a mineral called vermiculite. Put the soil in the box. Next, create a grid on the top of the box. Mark off 1-foot squares. You could use heavy tape stapled to the edges of the box.

Now the fun begins! Think about what fruits and vegetables you'd like to grow. Make a list. Then you should look up some facts about each type of plant.

READ! Like a Writer

Use one or more of the following questions to guide discussion about the writing traits in the article:

Sentence Fluency How does the writer use different kinds of sentences to make the article interesting to read? **Possible response: The writer uses questions, statements, and commands to make the text lively and interesting.**

Conventions How does the writer's use of proper grammar, punctuation, and capitalization help the reader understand the article? **Possible response: The article is easy to read and understand because the grammar, punctuation, and capitalization are correct.**

Sophia's Square Foot Garden Plan

basil	4 plants per square
beets	9 plants per square ①
bush beans	9 plants per square not beside onions
cantaloupe	1 plant needs 2 squares needs trellis
carrots	16 plants per square
garlic	4 plants per square
lettuce	1 plant per square
onions	16 plants per square not beside beans
peppers	1 plant per square
tomatoes	1 plant needs 4 squares grows tall needs cage
watermelon	1 plant needs 2 squares needs trellis

Sophia will grow her own square foot garden. She listed the plants she wants to grow and how much space they will need.

Find answers to these questions:
- Does this plant take up more than 1 square foot as it grows?
- If not, how many of these plants can grow within 1 square foot?
- Does this plant have trouble growing well near certain other plants?
- Does this plant need help standing up while it grows? (If so, plant it with a trellis or a cage on the outside of the garden.)
- Does this plant grow tall enough to cast a shadow? (If so, plan to put it on the north side of your garden.)

Once you answer these questions, you can see how to best use the space in your garden bed. Then you can plant seeds or small plants. Enjoy your fresh produce!

Cite Text Evidence

1. Use Text Features Use Sophia's garden plan to answer these questions.
- How many beet seeds does Sophia need to plant? Highlight the text that answers the question and label it 1. Write the answer below.
  9
- Why does she need these notes?
  in order to know how much space each type of plant needs

2. Analyze Images Use the illustration on page 34 to answer the questions.
- How many one-foot squares will fit in Sophia's garden?
  16
- Which plants need more than one square of space in her garden?
  watermelon, cantaloupe, and tomatoes

3. Quote Accurately What is the recipe for good potting soil? Highlight the text that answers the question and label it 3. Write the answer below and use quotation marks.
  "The recipe calls for equal amounts of compost, peat moss, and a mineral called vermiculite."

35

Cite Text Evidence (Teacher notes)

1. Use Text Features Explain that authors include text features, such as charts, to provide more information about the topic. In this article, the author includes a chart to show one person's plan for her own square foot garden.

2. Analyze Images Remind students to look closely at the images that accompany a text because they often contain important information. The image of the square foot garden shows where each plant will go and how many square feet of space each plant needs.

3. Quote Accurately Explain that it is important to use quotation marks when using a direct quotation, or the author's exact words. Tell students that quoting directly from a text is a good way to support a thought or idea they have about the text.

Academic Vocabulary

USE CONTEXT CLUES

Tell students they can use the context, or the words surrounding an unfamiliar word, to unlock that word's meaning. Point out the word *trellis* in the fourth bullet point on page 35. Ask students which words in the sentences are clues to the meaning of *trellis*. Guide them to understand that a trellis is a frame that helps a plant stand up while it grows. Its structure might contain a grid pattern like a cage.

Preteach Vocabulary

Resources for preteaching key vocabulary from this article can be found at **irtw.zaner-bloser.com**.

Student Objectives

- Solve mathematical and real-world problems.
- Critique and explain reasoning and solutions.

Apply Text Evidence

SOLVE MATH PROBLEMS Tell students they will now solve problems based on the article they just read. Read the questions on page 36 aloud to students or have them read the questions independently. Discuss any words or ideas they find confusing. Encourage students to review the evidence they gathered on the sticky notes and revisit the text for additional details to help them solve the problems.

A Garden Just for You!

Choose the best answer for each question below.

Solve the Problem

4. Sophia has $1.00. She decides to buy the beet seeds she needs. The seeds cost 10 cents each. How much money will she have left?
   - (A) 9 cents
   - **(B) 10 cents**
   - (C) 81 cents
   - (D) 90 cents

   Use Sticky Note 1

5. Which statement about Sophia's garden plan is true?
   - **(A) Its area is 16 square feet.**
   - (B) Its perimeter is 8 feet.
   - (C) The beets need 2 square feet.
   - (D) The tomato needs 8 square feet.

   Use Sticky Note 2

6. How much of the potting soil should be made up of compost?
   - (A) $\frac{1}{2}$
   - **(B) $\frac{1}{3}$**
   - (C) $\frac{1}{4}$
   - (D) $\frac{1}{5}$

   Use Sticky Note 3

36

Show Your Work

Responses will vary.

THINK! Like a Writer

Explain to students that the questions on pages 36 and 37 are designed to help them think about what the author had to say and what the structure of the text and its features tell the reader.

Point out that the questions on page 37 ask them to explain their reasoning.

Encourage students to ask themselves questions such as the following as they plan their responses:

- Did Cole understand what the problem was asking him to solve? If not, where did he get confused?
- Did I explain my reasoning clearly and use precise math words?
- Does my answer make sense?

Analyze and Respond

Possible responses appear below.

Use evidence from the text to answer each question below.

7. Cole answered question 4 by choosing C, 81 cents. How do you think Cole got that answer? Is his answer correct? If not, explain how to do the problem so he understands how to get the correct answer.

> **Cole probably got his answer by adding the number of seeds (9)**
>
> **to the cost (10 cents), and subtracting 19 cents from one dollar, but**
>
> **his answer is not correct. To get the correct answer, multiply the**
>
> **number of beet seeds needed by the cost (10 cents): 9 × 10 = 90**
>
> **cents. Then subtract 90 cents from $1.00: $1.00 - .90 = .10.**

8. How did you find the correct answer to question 5? Explain your reasoning.

> **I multiplied the number of square feet across the top (4) and down**
>
> **each side (4) to figure out the total area in square feet (16 sq ft).**
>
> **I multiplied one side (4 ft) times four to find the total perimeter**
>
> **(16 ft). I counted the number of square feet to determine the area**
>
> **needed to grow beets (1 square foot) and tomatoes (4 square feet).**
>
> **I realized that A was the correct answer.**

9. Sophia needs to mix 24 cubic feet of soil for her garden. How much of each type of ingredient does she need to make that much soil? Explain your reasoning.

> **Sophia needs 8 cubic feet of compost, 8 cubic feet of peat moss,**
>
> **and 8 cubic feet of vermiculite because the recipe calls for equal**
>
> **amounts of each ingredient: 24 ÷ 3 = 8.**

Students may draw a bar model like this:

24		
8	8	8

Explain Reasoning

ANALYZE AND RESPOND Tell students that they will now critique and explain answers to the problems they solved on page 36. Read the questions on page 37 aloud to students or have them read the questions independently. Discuss any words or ideas they find confusing. Point out that they may need to include evidence from the text to support their responses.

COLLABORATION

PEER GROUPS

Assign students to small groups to discuss and answer the questions on page 37 together. Have students take turns explaining to the group in their own words what they think each question is asking. Then have them explain their answers. After students have received feedback about their responses, have them write their responses independently.

READ!

Student Objectives

- Analyze a text source.
- Focus on domain-specific vocabulary.
- Cite evidence from the text.

Close Reading Process

FIRST READING Ask students to read the article independently to understand the main idea. As they read, have students mark any words or ideas they find confusing. Ask them to share words or ideas they found confusing. Then discuss the main idea.

Note: You may wish to read the article aloud to students, pointing out key vocabulary words and discussing their meanings as you read. Students may also read with a partner.

SECOND READING Ask students to reread the text, citing evidence as indicated on the sticky notes on page 39. Tell students that this evidence will be important as they solve the problems on pages 40–41.

WHAT A TREE!

by Deanne Kells

Meet General Sherman. Many people call it the largest living thing on Earth. Not everyone agrees on that, but it *is* the biggest *tree* in the world. It stands 275 feet tall. Its trunk measures 102 feet around at the bottom. And it weighs a whopping 2,700,000 pounds!

Wait . . . did you say "weighs"? How can you weigh a tree?

The answer is that you can't weigh a living tree—not on a scale. But there is a way for scientists to figure out how much a tree probably weighs. First, they measure its height. Then they measure its girth (the distance around its trunk) all up and down the trunk. They also need to know the area of its crown. The crown is the top part of the tree with leaves and branches. To find the area, you multiply the length of the crown by its width.

Next, they look up the tree's density. Think of density as how hard the wood is. A very hard wood weighs more than a soft wood. General Sherman is a giant sequoia tree, so scientists looked up the density number for giant sequoias.

Finally, they had to think about the limbs, branches, cones, buds, leaves, and flowers. These all affect how much a tree weighs.

With all this information, scientists used math to figure out how much General Sherman likely weighs.

For some people, it doesn't really matter. After all, General Sherman has been alive for more than 2,000 years. It's still growing. Year by year, bit by bit, it grows more wood. Its trunk gets wider, and its limbs get thicker. Over time, General Sherman will weigh even more than it does today!

38

READ! Like a Writer

Use one or more of the following questions to guide discussion about the writing traits in the article:

Ideas What information and examples support the main idea that General Sherman is the biggest tree in the world? **Possible response: The author includes facts, such as General Sherman's height and weight, to support the main idea.**

Organization What transition words does the author use to connect ideas in the text? **Possible response: The author uses the transition words *First*, *Next*, and *Finally*.**

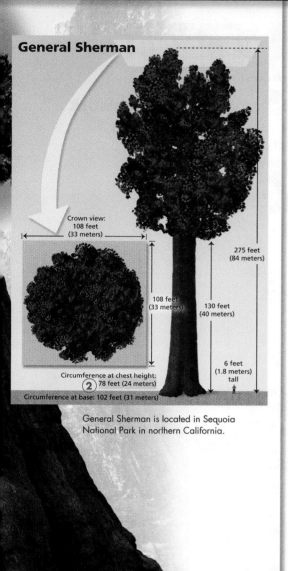

General Sherman

Crown view:
108 feet
(33 meters)

275 feet
(84 meters)

108 feet
(33 meters)

130 feet
(40 meters)

6 feet
(1.8 meters)
tall

Circumference at chest height:
② 78 feet (24 meters)

Circumference at base: 102 feet (31 meters)

General Sherman is located in Sequoia National Park in northern California.

Cite Text Evidence

1. Use Text Features Record the following details about General Sherman.

- Tree height:

  275 feet (84 meters)

- Circumference at the base (measurement around the bottom):

  102 feet (31 meters)

2. Use Text Features What is the measurement around the trunk at "chest height"? Use the illustration to answer the question. Highlight where you found the answer. Label it 2. Write the answer below.

78 feet (24 meters)

3. Ask and Answer Questions Think about how the tree's crown relates to the illustration.

- What do scientists need to know about the crown to figure out a tree's weight?

  The area

- How wide is the widest part of General Sherman's crown?

  108 feet (33 meters)

39

1. Use Text Features Tell students that labels in illustrations give additional information and details about the topic. In this article, the height, weight, and circumference of the tree are information provided in the illustration.

2. Use Text Features Explain that it is important to look closely at labels that accompany an illustration. Help students identify the label that indicates the tree's circumference at chest height.

3. Ask and Answer Questions Tell students that some questions they have about a text may be answered directly in the text, while others may require them to make an inference. Point out that the answers to both of these questions are stated directly in the text and in the illustration.

Domain-Specific Vocabulary

USE CONTEXT CLUES

Tell students that authors often include definitions or examples within a text to help readers better understand difficult concepts or unfamiliar terms. Point out the word *girth* in the third paragraph. Explain that the author includes a definition of *girth* after the word. Have a volunteer read the definition aloud. Invite students to look for other words that the author defines within the text. (*crown*, *density*)

Preteach Vocabulary

Resources for preteaching key vocabulary from this article can be found at **irtw.zaner-bloser.com**.

THINK!

Student Objectives

- Solve mathematical and real-world problems.
- Critique and explain reasoning and solutions.

Apply Text Evidence

SOLVE MATH PROBLEMS Tell students they will now solve problems based on the article they just read. Read the questions on page 40 aloud to students or have them read the questions independently. Discuss any words or ideas they find confusing. Encourage students to review the evidence they gathered on the sticky notes and revisit the text for additional details to help them solve the problems.

WHAT A TREE!

Choose the best answer for each question below.

Solve the Problem

4. Compare General Sherman's height to its circumference at the base. Which answer below shows how the two compare?

- Ⓐ 173 ft taller
- Ⓑ 377 ft taller
- Ⓒ 173 ft larger around
- Ⓓ 377 ft larger around

Use Sticky Note 1

5. If a man's reach is six feet, how many men his size are needed to reach around General Sherman's trunk at chest height?

- Ⓐ 12
- Ⓑ 13
- Ⓒ 17
- Ⓓ 20

Use Sticky Note 2

6. Which expression shows how to find the area of General Sherman's crown at its widest point?

- Ⓐ 108 ft ÷ 108 ft
- Ⓑ 108 ft + 108 ft
- Ⓒ 33 m × 108 ft
- Ⓓ 33 m × 33 m

Use Sticky Note 3

40

Show Your Work

Responses will vary.

THINK! Like a Writer

Explain to students that the questions on pages 40 and 41 are designed to help them think about what the author had to say and what the graphic tells the reader about the subject.

Point out that the questions on page 41 ask them to explain their reasoning.

Encourage students to ask themselves questions such as the following as they plan their responses:

- Did I solve the problem correctly? Does my answer make sense?
- Did I clearly explain my thinking? Can I add or change any words to make my thinking clearer?

Analyze and Respond

Possible responses appear below.

Use evidence from the text to answer each question below.

7. How did you solve the problem in question 4? Explain your reasoning.

I subtracted the girth of the tree at the bottom (102 feet) from the

total height of the tree (275 feet) to determine that the tree is 173

feet taller than it is around.

8. A classmate named Jeremy came up with "13 men" as the answer to question 5. He found the answer by subtracting 6 from 78 thirteen times. Is his answer correct? What is another way he could solve the problem?

Yes, his answer is correct. He could also solve the problem by

dividing the number of feet around the tree by the reach of each

man: $78 \div 6 = 13$.

9. How would the answer to question 6 change if it asked about a redbud tree with a crown that is 6 feet wide? Write the equation that shows how to find the area of the redbud's crown if it is evenly spread in all directions. Then solve the problem to find the area of the redbud's crown at its widest point.

6 feet × 6 feet = 36 square feet; The area of the redbud tree's crown

at the widest point is 36 square feet.

41

Explain Reasoning

ANALYZE AND RESPOND Tell students that they will now critique and explain answers to the problems they solved on page 40. Read the questions on page 41 aloud to students or have them read the questions independently. Discuss any words or ideas they find confusing. Point out that they may need to include evidence from the text to support their responses.

ENGLISH LANGUAGE LEARNERS

Math Word Bank Provide students with a word bank to help them write their answers to the questions on page 41. The word bank might contain math words such as *add*, *subtract*, *multiply*, and *divide* with the operation symbol beside each. You might also use sticky notes on the illustration of General Sherman to label words such as *height*, *circumference*, *base*, *crown*, and *area*.

WRITE!

Student Objectives

- Analyze the writing task.
- Write to multiple sources.

Analyze the Writing Task

IDENTIFY PURPOSE AND AUDIENCE

Explain that all writing has a purpose and is aimed at a specific audience. Read and discuss with students the different options for their writing projects, emphasizing the reasons or purposes for writing each genre and who the specific audience might be. Ask students to compare and contrast the purposes for writing within each genre.

Select a text type and genre for each student or invite them to read through the prompts on pages 43–45 and choose their own.

REVIEW THE WRITING PROCESS

Read and discuss each of the steps in the writing process. Point out that these are the steps students will follow as they write. Ask them to identify key points to remember for each step.

AVOID PLAGIARISM: PARAPHRASING

Explain that plagiarism is using another person's words *as your own* and does not represent good writing. Tell students that one way to avoid plagiarism is by paraphrasing, or using your own words and sentence structures to explain a concept or idea. Encourage them to write down the main ideas from sources as they take notes instead of writing information from the text word for word.

WRITE!

Analyze the Writing Task

You can write one or more of the following using information from the sources you read: a short story, a compare-and-contrast essay, or an editorial. Review the information below to understand each text type and genre.

Narrative

Short Story

A short story is a brief story that contains a full plot, at least one character, and some conflict that needs to be resolved.

The most common reasons to write a short story are to be creative and to entertain the audience.

Informative/Explanatory

Compare-and-Contrast Essay

A compare-and-contrast essay tells how two or more things are alike (compare) and different (contrast).

Reasons for writing a compare-and-contrast essay are to inform the audience about something or to evaluate two things to decide which is better.

Opinion

Editorial

An editorial is a piece of writing that expresses the author's opinion.

A good reason for writing an editorial is to convince readers to take action. If a writer is able to present an argument in a logical way, the audience will be more likely to take action.

The Writing Process

1 **Prewrite** Review the information you gathered and organize your ideas using a graphic organizer.

2 **Draft** Write your short story, compare-and-contrast essay, or editorial.

3 **Revise** Look for ways to improve your writing. Refer to the writing traits on page 46 as you revise.

4 **Edit** Check your writing for any errors.

5 **Publish** Share your writing with others.

Next Generation Assessment Practice

For additional practice with close reading and writing to multiple sources, use the **downloadable** Zaner-Bloser Next Generation Assessment Practice Tests. Modeled on the next generation assessments, the tests are designed to simulate an online test experience.

Writing to Sources
Narrative

Write a short story about two animal friends. One lives in a giant sequoia tree. The other lives in a square foot garden. Include a description of the settings. Use the articles as sources for your writing. Use the Story Map below to organize your ideas.

Writing Traits

Go to page 46 for a complete list of the **narrative writing** traits.

Story Map

Answers will vary.

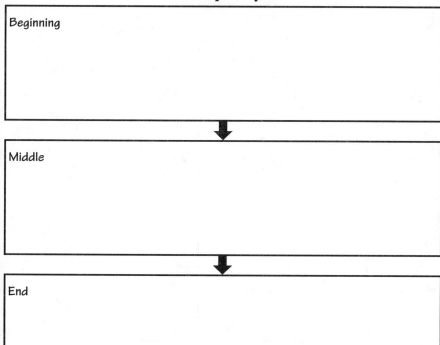

Beginning

Middle

End

43

Graphic Organizers

Additional graphic organizers can be found at **irtw.zaner-bloser.com**.

Use the Narrative Rubric

➤ Go to Page T48

The **Narrative** text-type rubric can be used by students to plan and improve their writing. It can also be used to assess students' writing. Point out that this rubric emphasizes the use of **precise description**, **sensory details**, and **logical event sequence to tell a story**. You will find more information about the text-type rubrics on page T47.

Writing to Sources: Narrative

1 PREWRITE Tell students they will now use the evidence they gathered from each source to write a short story about two animal friends who live in different places. Use the following questions to guide discussion:

- What information can I use to describe the settings?

- What details will make the characters come to life?

- What problem could the characters solve together?

Have students use the Story Map to organize their ideas.

2 DRAFT As students draft, remind them to keep their Story Maps out and refer to them frequently.

3 REVISE Have students refer to the chart on page 46 for a complete list of the narrative writing traits. Remind them to ask questions such as the following as they revise:

- Did I use descriptive details to tell about the settings and characters?

- Did I tell about the events in an order that makes sense?

4 EDIT Explain that during this step students should check their short story for any errors in spelling, punctuation, capitalization, and grammar.

5 PUBLISH Remind students that neatness counts. Discuss how word-processing software can help them publish an attractive final copy (e.g., choosing a simple font; using the tab key to indent paragraphs).

WRITE!

Writing to Sources: Informative/Explanatory

1 PREWRITE Tell students they will now use evidence they gathered to write a compare-and-contrast essay to explain how much space giant sequoia trees and garden plants need to grow. Use the following questions to guide discussion.

- What will my audience need to know about each type of plant?

- How is each type of plant different?

- Why are both types of plants important to people?

Have students use the Venn Diagram to organize their ideas.

2 DRAFT As students draft, remind them to keep their Venn Diagrams out and refer to them frequently.

3 REVISE Have students refer to the chart on page 46 for a complete list of the informative/explanatory writing traits. Remind them to ask questions such as the following as they revise:

- Did I introduce the topic clearly?

- Did I give facts and examples to support my main idea?

4 EDIT Explain that during this step students should check their essays for any errors in spelling, punctuation, capitalization, and grammar.

5 PUBLISH Remind students that neat presentation is important. Discuss how word-processing software can help them publish an attractive final copy (e.g., choosing a simple font; inserting photographs or illustrations).

T44

Informative/Explanatory

Compare and contrast giant sequoia trees and garden plants. Explain how much space these plants need. Use the articles as sources for your writing. Use the Venn Diagram below to organize your ideas.

Writing Traits
Go to page 46 for a complete list of the **informative/explanatory writing** traits.

Answers will vary.

Venn Diagram

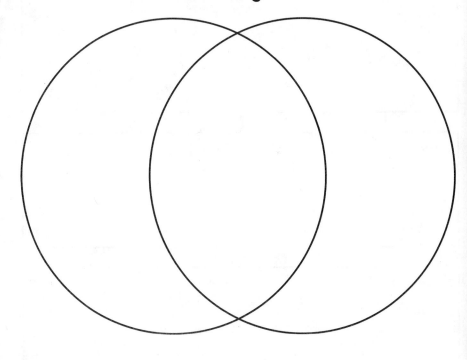

44

Use the Informative/Explanatory Rubric

➤ Go to Page T49

The **Informative/Explanatory** text-type rubric can be used by students to plan and improve their writing. It can also be used to assess students' writing. Point out that this rubric emphasizes the importance of including a **strong introduction**, using an **engaging voice**, and providing **clear transitions** that connect ideas. You will find more information about the text-type rubrics on page T47.

Opinion

Write an editorial that will appear in a newspaper. Your goal is to convince city planners that the city needs more forest hiking trails and community gardens. Use the articles as sources for your writing. Use the Support Pattern below to organize your ideas.

Writing Traits

Go to page 46 for a complete list of the **opinion writing** traits.

Answers will vary.

Support Pattern

Topic _____

Main Point _____

  Supporting Facts

  ➤ _____

  ➤ _____

  ➤ _____

Main Point _____

  Supporting Facts

  ➤ _____

  ➤ _____

  ➤ _____

45

Use the Opinion Rubric

➤ Go to Page T50

The **Opinion** text-type rubric can be used by students to plan and improve their writing. It can also be used to assess students' writing. Point out that this rubric emphasizes the importance of clearly introducing and supporting a **point of view** with logically ordered **reasons** and **information**. You will find more information about the text-type rubrics on page T47.

Writing to Sources: Opinion

1 PREWRITE Tell students they will now use the evidence they gathered from each source to write a newspaper editorial to convince others that their community needs more hiking trails in the forest and community gardens. Use the following questions to guide discussion:

• What are the reasons for having more hiking trails?

• What are the reasons for having community gardens?

• What facts and examples from the sources can I use to support my opinion?

Have students use the Support Pattern to organize their ideas.

2 DRAFT As students draft, remind them to keep their Support Pattern graphic organizers out and refer to them frequently.

3 REVISE Have students refer to the chart on page 46 for a complete list of the opinion writing traits. Remind them to ask questions such as the following as they revise:

• Is my opinion clear?

• Are my reasons and examples grouped in a way that makes sense?

4 EDIT Explain that during this step students should check their editorials for any errors in spelling, punctuation, capitalization, and grammar.

5 PUBLISH Remind students that neat presentation is important. Discuss how word-processing software can help them publish an attractive final copy (e.g., choosing a simple font, using the tab key to indent paragraphs).

	Narrative	Informative/Explanatory	Opinion
Ideas	• a topic that is just the right size, not too big or too small • descriptive details that answer the reader's questions (such as *who, what, where, when,* and *why*)	• a clear, focused topic • supporting details that are complete and accurate	• a clearly stated opinion • reasons that are supported by examples and details
Organization	• a logical sequence of events • a strong beginning and a satisfying ending • transition words that signal the order of events	• related information that is grouped in paragraphs • a strong introduction, body, and conclusion • transition words that connect ideas	• a strong introduction, body, and conclusion • organized paragraphs that stick to one main idea • transition words that show how ideas are related
Voice	• a voice that is friendly and speaks directly to the audience • dialogue that, if used, fits the characters	• a voice that sounds interested and informative and connects with the reader	• a voice that is clearly convincing and fits the writer's purpose • a tone that is appropriate and engages the audience
Word Choice	• exact words that tell the story • clear and precise nouns and verbs	• exact words that are appropriate for the reader • definitions for words that the reader may not know	• precise words and fair language that convince the reader • no unnecessary words
Sentence Fluency	• a variety of sentence lengths that makes the story flow smoothly	• clear, direct sentences • different sentence types and lengths to make the writing flow	• varied sentences that flow smoothly
Conventions	• no errors in spelling, grammar, punctuation, and capitalization	• no errors in spelling, grammar, punctuation, and capitalization	• no errors in spelling, grammar, punctuation, and capitalization

Using Rubrics for Instruction and Assessment

What is good writing? More specifically, which qualities of writing cause readers to be entertained, persuaded, enlightened, and informed? Excellent rubrics answer these questions by capturing the essence of a reader's expectations. In fact, the words of a well-crafted rubric may almost sound to a writer like advice from a trusted friend.

High-quality, trait-specific rubrics help students and teachers go far beyond simply evaluating the "correctness" of text. These indispensable tools enable writers to focus on the most impactful elements of composition as they prewrite, draft, revise, edit, and publish excellent writing. For these reasons and many more, *I Read to Write* incorporates exemplary text-type-specific, trait-based rubrics to support the development and assessment of student writing. These rubrics are found on pages T48–T50.

The same writing traits found in the text-type-specific rubrics can also be found embedded in the rubrics designed for the next generation writing assessments. Use the next generation assessment-inspired rubrics located in the *Zaner-Bloser Next Generation Assessment Practice* tests for additional support in preparing and assessing student readiness for the new assessments.

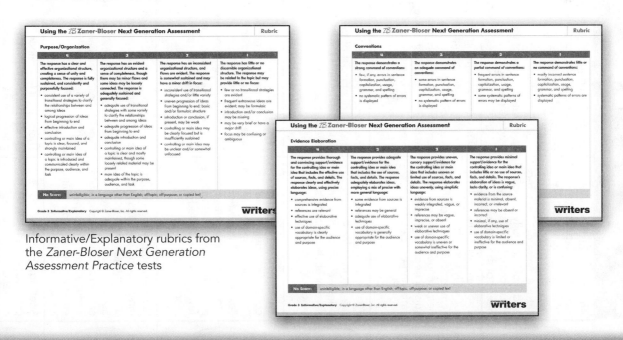

Informative/Explanatory rubrics from the *Zaner-Bloser Next Generation Assessment Practice* tests

Narrative Writing Rubric

	6	5	4	3	2	1
Ideas	The topic is just the right size—not too big or too small. Descriptive details introduce and develop the setting, narrator, characters, and plot. Carefully selected ideas completely satisfy the needs of the reader.	The topic is the right size. Most details introduce and develop the setting, narrator, characters, and plot. Carefully selected ideas satisfy most of the reader's needs.	The topic is the right size. Some details introduce and develop the setting, narrator, characters, and plot. The ideas selected by the author frequently meet the needs of the reader.	The topic is too big or too small. Some details develop the setting, narrator, characters, and plot. The ideas selected by the author sometimes meet the needs of the reader.	The topic is undeveloped. Too few details develop the narrative. Some details are unrelated. The author did not consider the needs of the reader.	The writing is not a narrative. Details are not included.
Organization	The narrative unfolds logically and naturally. Temporal words and phrases help sequence the events. A strong beginning leads to a satisfying conclusion.	One or two events in the middle are not connected or are out of order. Temporal words and phrases help sequence most of the events. The beginning or the conclusion is strong.	Some events are not connected or are out of order. Temporal words and phrases are needed to help sequence the events. The beginning and the conclusion work, but may not be strong.	The narrative does not unfold logically and naturally. Events are out of order. Temporal words and phrases are confusing or missing. The beginning or the conclusion is weak.	The narrative does not unfold logically. Events are out of order. Temporal words and phrases are not used. The beginning or the conclusion is missing or problematic.	The writing is disorganized and very difficult to follow. No beginning or conclusion is evident.
Voice	The voice, mood, and tone are just right for the purpose. Dialogue, if used, reveals each character's voice clearly.	The voice, mood, and tone are just right most of the time. Dialogue, if used, reveals the characters' voices.	The voice, mood, and tone are just right in places, but inconsistent. Dialogue, if used, somewhat reveals the characters' voices.	The voice sounds disinterested. Mood and tone are weak. Dialogue, if used, does not uniquely distinguish the characters' voices.	The voice, mood, and tone are not consistent. Dialogue, if used, does not sound right for some of the characters.	Voice is flat. Mood and tone are absent. Dialogue is not used.
Word Choice	Words and phrases consistently help the reader "see" the characters and "experience" the events. Nouns and verbs are clear and precise, supported by a few carefully selected modifiers.	Words and phrases frequently help the reader "see" most of the characters and "experience" most of the events. Nouns and verbs are mostly clear and precise. Most modifiers are carefully selected.	Some words and phrases help the reader picture characters and events, but some are too general. Certain nouns and verbs are weak, requiring too much help from modifiers. Modifiers are satisfactory.	Many words and phrases are too general. They keep the reader from picturing the characters and events clearly. Nouns and verbs lack clarity or precision. Too many or too few modifiers are used, and many of them are weak.	Most words do not help the characters and events come alive for the reader. Nouns and verbs are vague, unclear, or confusing. Modifiers may be missing entirely.	Many words are not used correctly. They distract the reader.
Sentence Fluency	Varied sentence beginnings, lengths, and patterns make the writing flow smoothly. Several particularly well-crafted sentences add style and interest. The paper is effortlessly read aloud with inflection or feeling.	Most sentence beginnings, lengths, and patterns are varied. One or two sentences add style. The paper is easily read aloud with inflection or feeling.	There is some variation in sentence beginnings, lengths, and patterns. The sentences are correct but ordinary. The paper can be read aloud with inflection or feeling.	Many sentences have the same beginnings, lengths, and patterns. This interrupts the flow of the writing. The sentences are mostly correct but ordinary. It is difficult to read the paper with inflection.	All or almost all the sentences follow the same pattern. Lengths and beginnings do not vary, making the writing robotic or rambling.	Sentences are poorly written or incorrect. The writing does not flow.
Conventions	Spelling, grammar, punctuation, and capitalization are correct. The narrative contains no errors.	There are a few minor errors, but they do not make the narrative difficult to read.	There are a few grammatical errors that may cause the reader to pause momentarily, but meaning is clear.	Many errors are present, and some confuse the reader.	Several serious errors make the narrative hard to understand.	The writing has not been edited.

Informative/Explanatory Writing Rubric

	6	5	4	3	2	1
Ideas	The topic is introduced clearly. Information and examples develop the main idea(s). Carefully selected ideas completely answer the reader's main questions.	The topic is introduced clearly. Most of the information and examples develop the main idea(s). Almost all of the reader's main questions are answered.	A topic is introduced. Some of the information and examples develop the main idea(s). The ideas chosen by reader's main questions are answered.	A topic is introduced, but information or examples do not develop the main idea(s). Some of the author did not think about what questions the reader might have.	A topic is introduced, but information and examples are incomplete or unrelated to the topic.	A topic is not introduced. Information and examples are incomplete or unrelated to the topic.
Organization	Information is organized into a strong and thoughtful introduction, a body, and a satisfying conclusion. Varied and appropriate linking words connect the ideas.	Information is organized into an introduction, a body, and a conclusion. Most linking words are varied and appropriate.	Information is organized into an introduction, a body, and a conclusion. More or better linking words are needed.	Information is not well organized. The introduction, body, and conclusion may be poorly developed. Linking words are confusing or not helpful.	Information is only partly organized. The introduction and conclusion is missing. Linking words are not used.	The writing is not organized. Introduction and conclusion may both be missing. Linking words are not used.
Voice	The voice sounds interested and informative. It fully connects with the audience and conveys the writer's purpose well.	The voice sounds informative and mostly connects with the audience. It conveys the purpose fairly well.	The voice sounds informative and connects with the audience somewhat. It conveys the purpose some of the time.	The voice sounds informative in places. It conveys the purpose, but often fades out.	The voice consistently sounds flat. It may sound uninformed or uninterested. It does not convey the purpose.	Voice is weak or absent. It does not connect with the audience or convey the writer's purpose.
Word Choice	Precise language and domain-specific vocabulary are used. Definitions are complete and helpful. Nouns and verbs are clear and precise, supported by a few carefully selected modifiers.	Precise language and domain-specific vocabulary are used. Most definitions are complete and helpful. Nouns and verbs are mostly clear and precise. Most modifiers are carefully selected.	Some precise language, domain-specific vocabulary, and definitions are used. Some nouns and verbs are weak, requiring help from modifiers. Modifiers are satisfactory.	Little precise language, domain-specific vocabulary and definitions are used. Definitions are missing or incorrect. Nouns and verbs lack clarity or precision. Too many or too few modifiers are used, and many of them are weak.	Some domain-specific vocabulary is used incorrectly. Clarification and definition are not provided for the reader. Nouns and verbs are vague, unclear, or confusing. Modifiers may be missing.	Precise language and domain-specific vocabulary are not used.
Sentence Fluency	Clear, concise sentences make the text flow smoothly. Sentence beginnings, lengths, and patterns are varied for effect. The paper is effortlessly read aloud with inflection.	Most of the sentences flow smoothly. The sentence beginnings, lengths, and patterns are varied. The paper is easily read aloud with inflection.	One or two sections of the writing do not flow smoothly. In these sections, several sentences may have the same beginnings, lengths, or patterns. The paper can be read with inflection.	In many places, the writing does not flow smoothly due to repetitive sentence beginnings, lengths, and patterns. It is difficult to read the paper with inflection.	All or almost all the sentences have similar beginnings, lengths, or patterns. The writing sounds robotic or rambling.	Sentences are incomplete or incorrect.
Conventions	The text contains no errors. Spelling, grammar, punctuation, and capitalization are correct.	The text contains very few errors in spelling, grammar, punctuation, or capitalization. The meaning remains clear.	The text contains some errors in spelling, grammar, punctuation, and capitalization. One or two errors may cause the reader to pause momentarily, but meaning remains clear.	The text contains many errors in spelling, grammar, punctuation, and capitalization. One or two errors interfere with meaning in places.	Many errors are present. Some errors are basic or repeated. The errors make the writing hard to understand.	Serious errors stop the reader frequently and make the writing hard to understand. The writing has not been edited.

Opinion Writing Rubric

	6	5	4	3	2	1
Ideas	The writer states a clear opinion. The perfect details and facts are chosen to support the writer's reasons.	The writer states a clear opinion. Most details and facts are well chosen to support the writer's reasons.	The writer states an opinion. Some details and facts are well chosen to support the writer's reasons.	The writer states an opinion, but few details are well chosen to support the writer's reasons.	The writer's opinion is not clear. Facts are inaccurate or unrelated to the writer's reasons.	The writer does not state an opinion. Reasons are not provided.
Organization	The text is organized logically and creatively. Helpful, appropriate, even unique linking words connect the writer's opinion and reasons. A compelling conclusion clearly supports the opinion statement.	The text is organized logically. One or two more linking words are needed to connect the opinion and reasons. The beginning is strong, and the conclusion supports the opinion statement.	The text is organized logically. More or better linking words are needed to connect the opinion and reasons. The beginning and the conclusion are functional. The conclusion relates to the opinion statement.	The text is not organized logically. Linking words may not show how the writer's ideas are related. Either the beginning or the conclusion is weak. The conclusion may not relate to the opinion statement.	The text is not organized logically. Linking words are not used. Ideas are hard to follow. The beginning or the conclusion is missing.	The text is not organized as an opinion. No beginning or conclusion is evident.
Voice	The voice is clearly convincing and totally fits the writer's purpose. The mood and tone are appropriate and engage the audience.	The voice is convincing and fits the writer's purpose. The mood and tone are appropriate and engaging most of the time.	The voice is somewhat convincing and fits the writer's purpose. The mood and tone are engaging some of the time.	The voice is convincing in some places. The mood and tone are incorrect or inconsistent. They lose the audience.	The voice is flat and does not fit the writer's purpose. The mood and tone do not engage the audience.	The voice is weak or absent. The tone is not appropriate.
Word Choice	Precise words and fair language convey the writer's opinion. No biased words or phrases are used. Nouns and verbs are clear and precise, supported by a few carefully selected modifiers.	Most words are precise and fair. No biased words or phrases are used. Nouns and verbs are mostly clear and precise. Most modifiers are carefully selected.	Some words are too general. One biased word or phrase may be used. Some nouns and verbs are weak, requiring help from modifiers. Modifiers are satisfactory.	Most words are weak. A few biased words or phrases may be used. Nouns and verbs lack clarity or precision. Too many or too few modifiers are used, and many of them are weak.	Many words are overused and ineffective. Several biased words and phrases are used. Nouns and verbs are vague, unclear, or confusing. Modifiers may be missing.	Words are weak, biased, or used incorrectly.
Sentence Fluency	A variety of sentence patterns adds interest and style. Great variation in sentence beginnings and lengths makes the writing flow very smoothly. The paper is effortlessly read aloud with inflection.	Most sentence patterns are varied and add interest. Variation in sentence beginnings and lengths makes the writing flow smoothly. The paper is easily read aloud with inflection.	Some sentence patterns are varied and add interest. Some variation in sentence beginnings and lengths is evident. The writing flows smoothly in some places, but not in others. The paper can be read with inflection.	Too many sentences share the same pattern. The writing does not flow smoothly due to a lack of variation in sentence lengths and/or beginnings. It is difficult to read the paper with inflection.	Almost all sentences are alike. The writing is boring and does not flow smoothly.	Sentences are poorly written or incomplete. The writing is hard to follow.
Conventions	The text contains no errors. Spelling, grammar, punctuation, and capitalization are correct.	The text contains very few errors in spelling, grammar, punctuation, or capitalization. The meaning remains clear.	There are some errors in spelling, grammar, punctuation, and capitalization. One or two of these errors may cause the reader to pause momentarily, but meaning remains clear.	Many errors are present. Some errors are basic or repeated. The errors interfere with meaning in places.	Serious errors stop the reader frequently and make the writing hard to understand.	The writing has not been edited.

INDEX